SMALL TALK

Discover How to Talk to Anyone and Make Friends

(How to Start a Conversation and Increase Self-confidence)

Alfonso Nickerson

Published By Andrew Zen

Alfonso Nickerson

All Rights Reserved

Small Talk: Discover How to Talk to Anyone and Make Friends (How to Start a Conversation and Increase Self-confidence)

ISBN 978-1-77485-343-6

All rights reserved. No part of this guide may be reproduced in any form without permission in writing from the publisher except in the case of brief quotations embodied in critical articles or reviews.

Legal & Disclaimer

The information contained in this book is not designed to replace or take the place of any form of medicine or professional medical advice. The information in this book has been provided for educational and entertainment purposes only.

The information contained in this book has been compiled from sources deemed reliable, and it is accurate to the best of the Author's knowledge; however, the Author cannot guarantee its accuracy and validity and cannot be held liable for any errors or omissions. Changes are periodically made to this book. You must consult your doctor or get professional medical advice before using any of the suggested remedies, techniques, or information in this book.

Upon using the information contained in this book, you agree to hold harmless the Author from and against any damages, costs, and expenses, including any legal fees potentially resulting from the application of any of the information provided by this guide. This disclaimer applies to any damages or injury caused by the use and application, whether directly or indirectly, of any advice or information presented, whether for breach of contract, tort, negligence, personal injury, criminal intent, or under any other cause of action.

You agree to accept all risks of using the information presented inside this book. You need to consult a professional medical practitioner in order to ensure you are both able and healthy enough to participate in this program.

TABLE OF CONTENTS

INTRODUCTION 1

CHAPTER 1: SHYNESS AND HOW TO OVERCOME IT 3

CHAPTER 2: ART SMALL TALK 10

CHAPTER 3: TECHNOLOGY & SMALL TALK 17

CHAPTER 4: SMALL TALK BEGINNING TALKERS 26

CHAPTER 5: THE REASONS SMALL TALK DOES NOT COME NATURALLY TO EVERYBODY 33

CHAPTER 6: SECRET OF RESTORING YOUR ENERGY 53

CHAPTER 7: BECOME MORE CONFIDENT IN CONVERSATIONS 61

CHAPTER 8: THE LITTLE TALK SKILLS THAT SET YOU APART FROM OTHER HUMANS 67

CHAPTER 9: TIPS ON INFLUENCING PEOPLE 80

CHAPTER 10: CREATING CONFIDENCE IN SMALL CONVERSATIONS 101

CHAPTER 11: LEARN HOW TO TALK ABOUT YOURSELF IN A RESPECTFUL MANNER 108

CHAPTER 12: UNDERSTANDING AND HOW TO DEAL WITH DIFFERENT KINDS OF CONVERSATIONALISTS 114

CHAPTER 13: SAFETY FOR SMALL TALK 127

CHAPTER 14: SMALL TALK ETIQUETTE 134

CHAPTER 15: TAKING IT TO THE NEXT LEVEL 140

CHAPTER 16: OPINIONS OF LEARNING 147

CHAPTER 17: TIME FOR THE TALKING BIT 152

CHAPTER 18: PREPARING YOUR MIND WITH A POSITIVE ATTITUDE 163

CHAPTER 19: WHAT TO DO AND DON'T'S TO AVOID WHEN YOU TALK TO A STRANGER 174

CONCLUSION 182

Introduction

The book "Small Talk" includes practical steps and strategies for how to conquer timidity, anxiety about social situations or even mild discomfort conversing with strangers!

It is impossible to realize how much someone could enhance your life or even how you can help your own by not talking to them! You might get to know someone special. ....Or simply imagine how many new friends you'd make if you simply chat with people whenever you're in public! Consider the benefits that you could enjoy professionally if it was not a problem to strike up an exchange with strangers.

If you've ever been uneasy engaging with other people, or simply being in the presence of other people If so, you're not by yourself. Many people feel uncomfortable engaging in conversations particularly when they have to talk to strangers. There are some who prefer to remain private and those who deliberately avoid interaction in contact with other people as much as they can.

Being human is just as much about social interaction than it does eating, breathing and sleeping. This means that for reasons of some kind or other you'll have to interact with individuals, meet people and have conversations correctly.

Chapter 1: Shyness and How to Overcome It

Shyness is not something you should be embarrassed of. While it's funny how it might be, we all experience the same feeling of being shy some way or another. Do you remember that you were required to appear before everyone in the group to present yourself? Perhaps you were required to stand before your boss and business partners to ensure you could present your presentation? What about the time when you were asked to deliver an address at your best friend's wedding, or on the anniversary of your parents?

If you are just meeting new people on the first occasion, it's common to experience anxiety which prevents people from sharing the correct words or keeps you wanting to escape as quickly in the fastest way you can. You are anxious and nervous and all you can do is wish you weren't there at all.

Many people are under the impression that only introverts suffer from shyness. People who are introverts tend to avoid social situations since they usually prefer to be alone instead of with others however, it's different from feeling the sensation of being shy. In contrast, shyness refers to the tendency to feel anxious or uncomfortable and occasionally nervous during social interactions. In most cases this feeling of unease is caused by encounters with strangers however it may also occur in various circumstances.

The concept of shyness can be detected by a variety of signs. Certain people who are shy may blush in the face of the awkwardness of a situation. In other cases, shyness can bring with it sweating, rapid pounding of the heart and the sensation of stomach discomfort. There are instances that shyness triggers lesser physical manifestations like that of someone who is shy, and they have negativity feelings concerning themselves. The people who feel shy are likely to be worried about how others might view their appearance or how other people perceive them, and so they are more likely to withdraw from social activities than to worry about people's perception of them.

Based on these statistics It isn't easy to discover that every person experiences some form of shyness at some moment throughout their life. The most confident of people may be shy when meeting the person of their goals, and even more shy about meeting the person's parents or relatives. A well-established businessman may be nervous when working with new partners or in addressing the shareholders despite the fact that they are highly respected and by others. Even the most renowned leaders are likely to be hesitant and unsure when faced with unanticipated praise or remarks.

In the end, there's no reason to be embarrassed in regards of being shy. It's a part of being human, like breathing is an integral aspect of living. If, however, you feel uncomfortable and are aware that your shyness is preventing you from doing what you need to do be doing, then something that must be completed. The good news is that there are more methods of conquering shyness than you think.

A feeling of shyness can result from feeling self-conscious, or worrying too much about what others may believe. In certain situations it can result in awkward social situations where the shy person stumbles or is unable to keep eye contact, or any kind of physical contact. However, in other cases it can cause a severe social phobia. The most frequent instances of shyness can be attributed to interactions with authorities such as bosses, teachers and even leaders, along with romantic relationships, and in various settings for groups.

Overcoming Shyness

People who want to conquer their shyness need to put all importance in understanding what shyness really is about. It isn't just about knowing the meaning behind shyness however, it is more about having a better understanding of the nature of their shyness. is.

Everyone is affected by shyness in their own manner. The reasons behind shyness vary in the manifestations and signs vary, and most importantly, the cause or cause of shyness can differ for each person. Before you start fighting your shyness, you must know more about the reasons behind it and how it comes about. When you understand the cause and the root of the problem, you have a greater chance of tackling the problem from the root and thus achieving better outcomes from the process of overcoming shyness.

There are three major reasons that people be shy. The first one is a low self-image. If you think of yourself as always not enough or often does things that aren't right most likely, you'll be constantly worried about others. However, what you feel about yourself or the things you think about doing often shows up in the world. So, if you think you'll commit a crime, most likely, you will.

But, it means that the answer is quite simple - put aside negative thoughts about your self! It's a lot easier said than done, but it's one of the best strategies to overcame shyness. Keep in mind that a self-image that is weak is nothing more than a voice in your head. It is, however, your mind and what you think. You can tell that voice to stop or, better yet let that voice speak something that is opposite to the negative thoughts that you're thinking.

Another reason people feel nervous is that they are aware of how they might appear to others. It is normal for humans to be aware of what others might be thinking about their appearance, but being incapable of functioning properly due to this isn't a great thing. The people who are shy for this cause will have to spend long hours working on themselves to appear attractive before others.

However they'll always be aware of every move they make, and whether or not they're making other people uncomfortable. The most simple way to deal with this is not to focus on oneself overly. Others are likely looking at other things in addition to yourself, and it is advisable to be doing the same.

In addition, some people tend to shy when other people think the shy are. When you're classified as shy, you have an increased likelihood to feel shy in social settings. Even if the person classified as shy is willing to fight back against the label however, the people who labeled them will continue to view them as shy. But, again, this is an issue of perception. What if people believe that you're shy? The more others believe that way, the more your motivation for showing them the opposite.

Each of these causes has some merit However, the main point is that you need to overcome these negative ideas if you are looking to overcome your shyness. Be positive about yourself Do not worry excessively about what others think of you and then let go of the opinions of others about your personality. The first step to overcome shyness is accepting that you're shy, understanding why this is, and then making a the intention of changing things around.

Chapter 2: Art Small Talk

When we think conversations with small people, it is easy to be thinking of not being interested in people we do not would like to talk to or even listen to an issue which is irrelevant. Small talk has, until now, actually serves a purpose to build relationships, personalities, and abilities. Talking about small talk can be described as the practice of creating a conversation people that you do not are familiar with and do not wish are ever going to get to know. For the majority of us, small talk us can be a stressful and uncomfortable moment. In the past, inability to talk about small things especially with strangers can affect our ability to communicate in our work environment, within the as well as with our community.

Thus when you feel awkwardly isolated from your friends and family members as you slog through the position that you have to put off for a few benefits of conversation that can make you feel more comfortable and break the ice.

Creates Network

When we conversations with strangers, we might make connections with others and, if lucky they could be a chance to start a an exciting new job or career and to find an outstanding service that we've sought out or even to make an acquaintance with the people we love. Small Talk could lead to networking opportunities. If your friend from small talk gives your name to other people and they do, they'll most likely give your contact information including your skills and experience. The power of small talk can be the most effective weapon for those who are operating a business of networking.

As an example I am a tech knowledgeable person. I also have plenty of experience with computers that I utilize as a hardware service freelancer to earn. My closest friends, colleagues my family, and a few clients I offered my services to are aware of it. In small talk, they may mention your name to others people, which will increase the number of contacts that you are part of and allow you to conduct more business transactions, and increase the amount of money you earn.

You'll be smarter

Small talk is crucial because it makes you more knowledgeable. It helps you become smarter as conversations are flowing, both you and the other person in the conversation share ideas and information that are more often if the topics are of interest to you. A study conducted by researchers of University of Michigan University Of Michigan found that an enjoyable social interaction increases our ability to resolve issues. As per Oscar Ybarra, the psychologist who was the researcher, the study revealed, "Some social interactions induce individuals to look into the minds of others and consider their own perspective on issues." A case that I came across in a brief conversation to a driver of a taxi when travelling, and was wondering "why the crude oil price is falling so quickly." The driver then asked me in a polite manner, "Boss, do you know the reason why the price of crude oil is declining since the 4th Quarter of the year 2014?" In a simple way to which he responded "It is falling as a result of OPEC Saudi Arabia has high supply, and less demand. Because the US is the largest consumers, US increase its output of locally-owned crude oil drilling firms. There is a sudden rise in demand for China use of crude oil. China assists in manipulating the price of OPEC Saudi Arabia oil product to fall." This is the question I asked the answer to me. I was able to gain an understanding of what's happening to the global crude oil market. If I ever have to ask the similar question, I can provide the right person to ask it.

It can inspire you and other people.

Small talk can lead to a fascinating conversation which will have a positive impact to your everyday life and may last for the rest of your life. Last December my wife and I attended a Christmas celebration and came across a minimalist businessman by engaging in a small talk.

We were able to begin a conversation. He was business partner along with my wife's boss.

He discussed how to live a an easy life and to eliminate clutter that does not support our pursuit of happiness. He also advised us that spending more attention and importance to the things that matter in life like family relations and less money spent by getting rid of material possessions can help us make our lives more enjoyable, build a career and achieve our goals to live a better life than we have previously. The most inspiring thing was that my wife and I came to an agreement for our new Year resolution to eliminate our home of clutter. Through donating them to our friends and strangers who require the items that isn't useful to us. It also decreases our spending every day and led to a greater savings in the bank within one month.

If you present yourself as open to new communication and conversations You could end being able to help someone else you did not knew needed assistance. I remember the taxi driver who I encountered while riding in his cab. I talked for three minutes, then began talking with me regarding his issues and his family's issues. We talked about the duration of my destination. After that, I didn't see him again. I remember the feeling of satisfaction that I had provided someone with compassion and positive words to help to ease the pain as the car left was pleasing to be able to observe. A chance meeting with someone who feel like they're without other person to talk to can change their lives, and allow them to release their emotions or assist them to deal with difficult thoughts by talking about their thoughts in a clear way.

It's inevitable.

Interviews, talking to coworkers, signing business agreements and entertaining your friends and family All require the ability to engage in small conversations. To be part of a larger community, you must also engage in small-talk. To become a successful leader, businessman and a great employee, you have to engage in small conversations. Talking about yourself is an instrument in all situations in our lives.

Chapter 3: Technology & Small Talk

It's becoming more and more common to send a text message to people who are making their initial contact, whether receiving a business card or calling the person you were referred to by. The use of technology could be a means to stay clear of small talk since you can sit and contemplate what you'd like to say without having the added tension of having someone stare at you. This could be viewed as beneficial and detrimental and it's nice to avoid awkward situations, however it could affect someone's social skills.

As per an article in the Harvard Business Review we're thirty-four times more effective in face-to-face conversations than texting.

The Pew Research Center "Heavy text users are more likely to choose texting over calling. Around 55% of the people who send more than 50 messages per day say they would prefer to receive a text message than a call."

There is a rising trend among younger generations to stay away from social interaction and instead turn towards technology according to the studies.

"Young adults are the biggest texters by a significant margin. Cell phone owners between 18 and 24 send the equivalent of 109.5 messages in a typical day. This translates to more than 3,200 text messages every month. On average, the average cell owner within this age bracket receives or sends 50 texts every week (or 1500 messages per month)."

If we give us such a powerful method to avoid conversations by texting, we're missing the most important aspects of conversations. There are many aspects that take place during conversations such as body speech as well as tone of voice and facial expressions we cannot see in a text message. This makes us interpret the meaning a person intended to convey a message, that, for me, has led to some wacky arguments that were not meant to be from the start. Every conversation we engage in with one another helps us get better at interpreting these signs and allows us to engage in more conversation that is natural. This is certainly a large element of social anxiety disorders and mental health issues that are prevalent in our modern society. Texting is the most popular method of communicating with other people for the generation of millennials, that causes you to consider how they're going to raise their children. It's not that millennials will not suffer from social anxiety, but if they are born into a culture in which social anxiety is increasing and getting more severe, it will become difficult to stay out of. The most effective tool available is to inform the millennial generation about the challenges that we face today, so that people aren't passing the issues to their children. We may be losing crucial conversational skills that the children require simply by throwing a tablet or phone before them. A lot of people depend on this in the present, and in the pre-cell phone age, placing children front of the TV was commonplace, but just because it was common practice before doesn't mean it's the right way to do it. Some may not be in agreement with me, but as a non-parent I can accept your objections of these practices, however, at the same time it's worth a look.

The paradox of technology allowing us to communicate with more people , and frequently causing problems with our everyday conversations isn't missed by me. A MIT professor in her most recent book wrote that "89 percent Americans claim that in their last social encounter they used phones". Additionally "82 percent believe that it negatively affected the conversation they had been in". This to me is one of the "duh" moments, but until people actually look it up, there are times when they don't know. It's a common belief that the use of phones is tied to self-control. As with many things, we should use them in moderation. It is not necessary to continuously look up the time, check whether we're getting an email or check out what this person has to say on the internet. It's important to stop and allow yourself to just be in the present and take in the moment. It's not long before we leave this planet and certainly do not want to spend the entire day staring in the screen.

The presence of a cell phone could reduce our compassion for the person we are communicating with, according to the results of a study from 2014. Because cell phones are still a relatively new technology, people have yet to figure out what they mean by the impact they have on everything. There are tons of surveys and polls , however the evidence for psychological effects cannot be compiled in a matter of hours. Today, all data is being closely monitored and tracked, and we have to be hopeful that the data will be employed for good purposes and not just for the most lucrative advertiser. We are adapting to technological advances, but our methods of dealing with them might not be the most effective. We also require more help regarding social anxiety and mental health issues that can be difficult to identify because everyone is on access to a mobile phone, and the research that doesn't point to everyone in need of assistance. What are the signs that you require help with your mental health? How can you tell if you suffer from social anxiety? Some people are more self-aware than others and it is difficult for people who are not as self-aware to acknowledge their mistakes.

Google Duplex along with the AI Revolution

This raises interesting subjects. With Google recently announced and releasing Google Duplex it will, in a sense it will simplify our lives since mundane tasks are handled with artificial intelligence. It's great to be able concentrate our attention on the most important issues instead of, as small conversation is described as "conversation over irrelevant topics" and we are experiencing an increasing number of mental health problems across many countries.

As per Mental Health America 18% of adults suffer from mental health problems. This means that more than 43 million Americans and 9.6 million are prone to the thought of dying. These issues are mostly without treatment as 56% didn't receive any treatment and 7.7 percent of adolescents are not able to access medical assistance for their mental health. Over a five-year period, the rates of depression among young people have dramatically increased. The rate has gone from 5.9 percent to 8.2 percent in those five years. It may seem like much, but when you consider the millions, that's an enormous amount. Health professionals who specialize in mental health must treat more than six times the number of people living in the lower of the states to be able to compete with those in higher-ranked states. This is a huge difference. The rise in technology utilized to avoid face-to-face discussions is reportedly tied to mental health issues growing.

While we're making use of the "phones" more often, we're using them for purposes apart from talking, like Instagram and facebook. This creates the appearance of social interaction, however it actually, it's the reverse. The internet's world of people can be quite deceiving, since people like to highlight only the positive and wonderful things they're accomplishing. It's easy to believe that others have flawless lives and we're one who is struggling, and looking at ourselves in comparison to the other people that we see on social media. This puts us in an unending cycle of "why should my life not be as good as theirs" and can lead to depressive thoughts and even more. We need to be aware that everyone has their own issues and, honestly, being alive is awe-inspiring.

There are a few concerns regarding the advantages and drawbacks of artificial intelligence being incorporated into our lives. Do we really need our smartphones to make appointment times and reserve restaurants? These may seem like routine tasks however, in a time when so many are suffering from mental health issues, do we really want to cut off the possibility of social interaction in their lives? Artificial Intelligence isn't going away therefore we must harness our adaptive nature and accept it. Also, we must create methods for dealing with mental health problems which are becoming more prevalent. I'm not sure if this will come off as sarcastic, but it's not meant to be. But with mental health concerns rising with artificial intelligence becoming commonplace, there will be plenty of opportunities for business. It's not my intention to say that it's ideal to earn money from mental health issues however if we can make a system to help people receive the assistance they require as a business I'm all in for it. We should be introducing alternative social interactions into all the social interactions that we're eliminating.

Chapter 4: Small Talk Beginning Talkers

There aren't many people who have an erupting self-confidence right at the start. Social skills are only sharpened by regular exposure to it which is, in essence that you have experiences. Nobody can become proficient at small talk unless they are able to practice the skill regularly in different scenarios. The more you practice it, the more adept you'll become at watching others and playing with topics that are light until you hit the perfect pitch that causes them to engage with the conversation with.

If you've been involved in conversation with others before but had disappointing (or worse, mediocre) outcomes, then these simple tips can to make it easier for you to socialize with new acquaintances and strangers:

1. Introduce yourself. Today, everyone has the liberty to introduce themselves, rather than being dependent on someone else's introduction to their friends. There's no

better method to introduce yourself to people at the social setting than to meet someone in person and extend your hand smile, make eye contact. Then, introduce yourself by saying, "Hello, my name is Bob. I am glad meeting you." Is it like a lot of work? Begin by thinking about people as potential friendships or clients , rather than worrying that they won't warm to you. Nothing will be lost by making an effort.

* Request the "expert opinion". If you are able to form an opinion about what someone else does for a living it is possible to ask for their opinion about what they are skilled at. For example, you can inquire from a salesperson on how she convinces clients to purchase her product or converse with the chef and ask the chef what secrets he has about how he can make his food taste so delicious. This is a great opportunity to improve your small talk abilities on a regular basis.

Create an interesting list of subjects. It could be a thought or a pencil and paper listing of subjects you enjoy talking about.

When you are done with your list, the best thing you can utilize it for small conversations is to begin with questions like "Did you know about that? ..." is a fact?" or "I found out from someplace about... What is your take on it?"

Try interviewing yourself for the first time. It may sound odd however it's actually an effective method of increasing your confidence. It is especially beneficial for people who are hesitant to have a conversation due to their fear of not being able to give honest and accurate information about themselves. Consider the kinds of questions that people typically pose in casual conversations like "what are you doing for an income?", "what are you proficient doing?", "how's your family?" and so on. It is possible to create responses to these questions before you ask them or note them down so that you can absorb them so that you'll have answers in hand that will not cause you to stumble.

* Be more attentive. Look around and assess your mood overall. This will help

you stay calm and doesn't cause you to worry too much. The observations you've made could allow you to have conversations with other people like declaring, "this party has a wonderful theme! Do you know who that came up with the idea?" or "Do you know who the man wearing the Nirvana shirt is? He looks familiar to me."

* Speak to at minimum one person every week. The ability to expand your social circle can be a boon starting by engaging your acquaintances and strangers with a casual conversations. This can allow you to build relationships, become significant business partners, as well as long-term customers. It could also open doors for you , such as making new acquaintances and getting new experiences. If the setting is considered safe (such as at a social gathering) it is safe to start chatting with others.

Join organizations. There are many social networks that are filled with people looking to build networks or just making new friends. Join a community and begin building your social skills right there. It's easy to join an environment that has the same interests.

Small Talk Starters for Business

Here are some simple conversation starters that you could apply to business interactions:

* What's your typical day at work like for you?
* What do like the most about your work?
* What was the inspiration behind you to develop an concept (for the business)?
* Can you talk to me the most difficult element of your career?

How did you begin your journey in this industry or field of work?

* What do you believe is the most effective method to promote your business?

What are the best tips you can give someone who is just beginning in your company?

* What are the most significant modifications or improvements your business has experienced?

Do you have someone within your business who can assist (me to market my product/teach me how to use the software I'm using, etc.)?

Small Talk Starters at Social Gatherings

Here are a few simple questions that you can utilize in order to get people talking virtually any social gathering:

* What was your favorite holiday you've ever taken?

What's your take regarding the food/decoror music/film?

What is the best way to get to know the host/hostesses?

* What do you normally do during hot and rainy days such as this?

• What consider to be the ideal age for an individual's life?

Which family tradition do you typically take part in during this holiday season?

• Who's your most favorite actor, actress, or singer. ?

* What are your most fond memories you've had with (someone whom you shared a common bond with)?

* Do you have any recommendations for an excellent restaurant, movieor shop at this location?
• What's the best food you've ever tried?
* If you could alter something about the location What would it be?
* What was the atmosphere in the area that you grew up in?
What was your favorite place to have your summers in the childhood?
"What do you consider to be the most romantic or funny film of the last decade?

Chapter 5: The Reasons Small Talk Does Not Come Naturally to Everybody

The human race is not an all-inclusive package. They each have their own personality and different reactions to the same stimulus, and different expectations, and often alter opinions at the touch of a button. It is impossible to predict the outcome you'll get prior to making contact with someone to discuss a topic.

The person could be suffering from an awful day and may be rebuking your actions even if you approach them with great intent and body language that gives security. Someone could be uncomfortable in social situations and has emotional barriers that prevent their ability to connect with other people. The way they appear on the outside could signal the opposite of any conversation, regardless of whether they require the connection. There are numerous negative results that can result when someone approaches you to talk about small issues.

However, the possibilities for positive outcomes are equally impressive.

It is possible to make a new acquaintance or discover something you never knew about and make a professional acquaintance or find out about an opportunity that you could benefit from.

A shy person tends to focus on the negatives that could happen and calculates the possibility of positive outcomes as being very small even for those they are familiar with. For someone like this, everyday encounters like speaking to people at the supermarket checkout could be a stressful encounter even if it's done in just a few minutes. Even everyday interactions such as making friends with strangers on the street or having a chat with friends from school are difficult. The truth is while the reasons for the discomfort are not resolved the situation is going to continue to happen.

If you're shy or awkward in social situations due to any reason, I'd like to inform you that you're an amazing creative, interesting and gifted person. There's no problem with who you are. The reason you are shy could be due to circumstances, genetics,, or just because you perceive things differently than others. Its cause is not of any significance right now. As you read the book you are aware the issue that has you in a bind and you're taking steps to eliminate the roadblock within your own life.

Before we begin to show the tricks, tips and strategies that can assist you in becoming an effective social communicator Let's take some time to discuss the reasons why shyness is keeping your back. Then, consider how you can overcome this issue, before speaking to someone else.

Understanding Shyness: The Reasons It makes Social Interactions a challenge

The stigma of shyness should not be taken as a boogeyman hiding beneath your mattress. It's not something to shame yourself about, or to be ashamed of. It's simply an aspect of many characteristics you have.

In actual fact there are many good benefits of being shy by nature. The majority of shy people are critical in their thinking before they behave. People generally view the shy person as reliable and modest, as well as great listeners and pleasant being around. This is why you should pick the traits of shyness you would like to keep, and those that you'd like to eliminate or change.

It is commonplace to confuse shyness with introversion. Both aren't one at all. While being introverted may indicate shyness however, introversion (and extrovert) is a part of one's personality that is linked to satisfaction with emotions. There are many introverts who aren't shy. They're not scared to interact with other people or have conversations. They can even be thriving when socializing. They will be drained of their energy when they are in crowd for most people. Although extroverts benefit due to their social interactions but they also have shy extroverts who have the usual shy signs. They might be more adept at hiding their shyness.

Another erroneous notion concerning shyness is it's often associated with lack of interest.

Shyness is a feeling that is characterized by insecurity, discomfort and self-consciousness. The physical manifestations of that emotion can be breathlessness, inability of speaking or talk, sweaty palms, shakiness and the appearance of blushing. As with all emotions, people feel these in different degrees and range from mild to extreme. In addition, the intensity may depend on other variables like the specific situation and the person that the shy person is with. Intense shyness usually completely destroys the person's capacity to be socially successful. This happens due to the fact that it damages their confidence in themselves and self-esteem.

In the world of so much misinformation on shyness, it's difficult to find the assistance needed to overcome it.

Being able to overcome shyness and living lifestyle to its fullest an all-encompassing process that addresses every one of the three issues that prevent you from becoming an effective social communicator and living a fulfilled social life.

1.) Understanding how to manage the stress and anxiety associated with shyness.
2.) Ending this cycle of avoidance and social isolation.
3.) Enhancing confidence in yourself.

Each of the three obstacles are equally important and we will address each one individually in this book.

Anxiety, regardless of its root cause, will take the same shape. While it can appear overwhelming and difficult to conquer However, there are strategies that you can implement to control anxiety. Take note that every strategy described below is best suited to various people and in various combinations. Therefore, experiment to find the best option for you.

Strategies to overcome anxiety associated with Social interactions

- Practice breathing slowly. Breathing patterns that are rapid and uncontrolled are indicators of shyness. If you control your breathing, you can put your shyness under control. Make sure you are able to move air in the direction of lung. Inhale deeply , and keep your breath in for three seconds. Exhale and hold for a count of three. Repeat this process until you breathe has returned to a normal rate.

* Work on muscle relaxation. Stress is a result of tension in your muscles. If you can reduce tension, you'll be able to be able to enjoy your time. Before you engage in any social activity make sure you are in a peaceful area, shut your eyes and loosen you muscles. Do this in a structured method. Start with your head, and then work your way to your toes.

* Be present in the moment. The shy typically dwell in their heads. They try to make an idea of what the future holds to limit the events that happen since they're not sure. The most important thing to enjoy the social interactions you participate in is to prevent from doing this.

Let your mind go and be present and active in what's happening. Engage in actively shutting off the part of your brain that keeps you from the present and return to where you are.

* Monitor your self-talk. Self-talk refers to the internal conversation that takes place within your mind. The self-talk could be positive, for instance "I am doing really well" however, it can be (and in fact, has a strong probability of becoming negative if not properly monitored) very negative. Self-talk that is negative can include "I am a slob at that" or "I do not have the skills."

* Keep a diary. If you are more conscious of the emotions occur when you're scared or nervous and unable to control these feelings. Do not rely solely on your memory as the mind is a flimsy thing. Instead, you should keep a journal and record what you feel when you're worried. Write down the emotions you experience when you've managed to conquer these feelings. When you reflect on these written notes, you will be able to find the strength to persevere.

Small social acts. In the absence of socializing you'll never be able to overcome your fear. Avoidance will only provide short-term relief, but you're hurting yourself in the long run. Thus, you should feed yourself tiny amounts of socialization until you are able to build yourself into a regular consumption of it. The brains of our minds transform those things we fear into gigantic monsters. Through small moments of socialization, it is possible to discover that the fear you are experiencing is exaggerated. After that, you can take additional steps towards your progress.

Be kind to yourself. There will be moments that you fail. It is possible to get tongue tied or make a mistake at the wrong moment. Perhaps, you won't even leave your house to a gathering. Accept the situation and don't smear yourself. Consider it an accomplishment and make plans to improve next time.

* Find others who are like you. You're just one of many shy people suffering from anxiety. Look for others with the same

issues and have a chat with them. This is not just an opportunity to socialize and interaction, but you'll feel less lonely and build relationships that last for a long time.

Avoid Avoidance

The shy typically prefer solitude to manage the feelings of anxiety, even when they are in need of intimacy and a sense of belonging to others. It could be that they have developed an habit that frequently leads to extreme solitude. It is certainly not healthy, and it is in complete contrast of what is needed to manage shyness effectively.

The natural response to avoidance is however it can keep us focused on the things that trigger anxiety. It creates fear. Moving past this obstacle requires taking action. Instead of avoiding it is important to put yourself in situations with which you're uncomfortable. This will be the sole way to improve and grow. It's not that you shouldn't overflow your life with stimulation from social networks. Slow down, but remain focused.

As an example, a great first step is to get out of your home and exploring your neighborhood. Begin by greeting the people you meet. Smile at them. If you happen to encounter them, ask them what they're doing. If a conversation arises from this, don't get caught up in it. Just follow the flow. Pay attention to whatever the person in question is saying and then respond with kindness. Focus on the person in question as well as ask them questions. Most people enjoy people who show interest in their interests. Make the conversation short and keep going. Repeat this process regularly, even if you don't feel like doing it, and you'll discover that you will be gradually more comfortable.

In this case, you should extend your excursion beyond your local area. Take a trip to the mall, coffee shop or other locations in which you can be exposed to people you haven't met before. Start by looking into the eyes of other people and say hello.

The most amazing things happen outside your comfortable zone. Get out of your comfort zone and engage. It may be challenging initially, particularly when your shyness is strong however, time, consistency and persistence are the key to overcome any obstacle.

When you are more at ease, you'll notice that your anxiety will lessen.

Have confidence in your social ability

Confidence isn't something that people have naturally. It is a learned set of behaviours that can improve your life quality. If you're shy You don't have to suffer with confidence issues. In the next section, we'll discuss the definition of confident in yourself and ways to increase your confidence.

Asperger's syndrome and how it makes effective small talk difficult

We've done a fair amount of time focusing on the issue of shyness in relation to efficient communication and social interactions because it's a very common problem that hinders effective small-talk. But, there are many other obstacles between you and your goals.

As we've mentioned before that genetics play an enormous influence on the ability to socialize, as is the case those with Asperger's syndrome. It is an empathetic form of autism. The majority of people with a form of autism are troubled with social interactions. The reason for this is that the brains of these individuals are wired in a different way than people who are a "normal" individual. This wiring difference often implies that they are unable or aren't as able to discern between the lines or recognize nonverbal messages as people of average age do.

What a normal person might be in a position to detect in a conversation, a person suffering from Asperger's Syndrome might not be capable of. The reason is that empathy is a characteristic they do not have. It is the capacity to comprehend the mood of another and respond accordingly. It isn't meant to mean that people who suffer from Asperger aren't compassionate but that dealing with emotions can be difficult for them.

The way that people who have Asperger's Syndrome socialize differs from other people with autism. People with autism are generally assumed to be passive within social settings. However, this is not true for those with Asperger's Disorder.

They often want to make friends and yearn for social interactions. However, their approach is likely to be awkward since they do not have the knowledge of how to make their exchange relaxing. Because they are unable to process emotional and social cues from their peers the conversation, they could come off as a bit pushy, insensitive or even a bit odd.

Small talk is comprised of a lot of non-verbal signals, something that could be more important than the words spoken. This is why it's obvious why people who suffer from Asperger's Syndrome are prone to having difficulties. Fortunately, they're not doomed to a lifetime of social isolation. They can be taught how to react more effectively to social cues, and even practices like small conversation.

The hacks that are listed and elaborated upon in this book will those who are shy in their socialization and communication abilities, they assist those who have a diagnosis these characteristics on the autism spectrum.

How to Enhance Your Social Skills If You Are Asperger's Disorder

The circumstances of people who have Asperger's Syndrome distinct and, therefore we've added some additional tips to assist them on the way to improved social and communication skills.

First of all, if you're an individual who struggles with social skills, or lack of them the latter, you must accept the fact that you might not be able to grasp the social concepts that are easily understood by other people. This isn't to suggest that you are inferior to others or that you have to see yourself as a handicapped person. Your perspective is different and that's the thing that makes life interesting. You see things in an completely different way. There are different values and you view things from a different angle.

Accept the difference and make use of the difference to benefit yourself rather than trying to fight it. Your quirky personality can add a unique flavor to conversations, which can make you memorable. In addition, acceptance of your differences lead to an interesting conversation, it can make you more happy as well.

You don't have to be affected by this condition, so do not allow it to rule your life. Don't let it be the reason why you don't attempt to develop your social abilities. To live life to the fullest is about self-improvement for everyone living on the planet. Asperger's Syndrome can present difficulties, and it can make it difficult to socialize. Consider it as a personal issue that others suffer from. If someone is struggling with problems with weight, then that person must consider the best approach to the issue of weight control. This is the same for those with Asperger's syndrome. Assess the strengths you have since you indeed possess them, and the same for your weak points. When you are aware of and comprehend these, you will be able to make the necessary changes to make use of those strengths for your benefit, and to reduce your weaknesses.

It is possible that you will need to approach the improvement of your social and communication abilities in a different way than the typical person. Be aware of this. If one approach or method doesn't work for you, you must learn what you can learn from it and proceed. Don't dwell on the mistakes or try to internalize your failure.

There could be lots trials and errors and. Put yourself in more situations that give you the chance to gain knowledge and improve your communication. You'll fail at certain situations, but you'll win in other. You'll always be able to gain knowledge regardless of whether it is something that is accepted by society or something to help to approach social interactions from a different viewpoint.

You could also play the role of the social skills group. This lets you experience specific social situations prior to when you meet these situations in real life. Then, you can practice the right responses and words to use. Groups for social skills training are generally something children who have Asperger's Syndrome are able to attend, however adults can benefit as well since activities that focus on small talks along with other interpersonal skills is often a part of.

The most important aspect is to continue making progress. This can be the only method to increase your performance. Slow and steady win the race.

It is also possible to seek assistance from an expert in social skills. This could be a family member , or someone you know who is capable of socializing and communicating well or even an experienced psychotherapist. You could try to emulate the behaviour of the person you are studying and seek their guidance when you need clarity on social interactions. They may also be able to give feedback on your social skills to help you are aware of the areas that you're required to work on as well as the areas that you are excelling in.

One thing you can be confident about when you struggle with social interactions because of the Asperger's Syndrome is that social interaction is a tolerant art. Although it is a process that involves numerous unspoken rules, and usually provides a suitable approach to dealing with certain situations, there's plenty of to allow for actions and communications that are good enough to ensure that the interaction does not end in a complete failure.

So, even though there are certain standards of conduct that an individual should behave in a social setting but a deviation from the norm will always mean the experience is not a success. It is possible that you are naturally explicit in your communicating, which could cause some people to be offended however that does not mean you can't convey your message or that it can't be effective in all situations. Knowing this will assist you in developing more subtle or tactful approach to use in the future.

Another suggestion is to let people inform them about your Asperger's. This can be a bit controversial because some people might not comprehend the issue and may react negatively, which makes the situation even more difficult for everyone concerned.

On the other hand this could make other people more accepting and understanding in any aspect of communication which you fail in. I suggest letting people be aware of your Asperger's condition in situations where there are repeated interactions.

Chapter 6: Secret of Restoring Your Energy

This chapter is geared towards introverts and those who often feel exhausted after any event or party either both physically and mentally. If you find yourself feeling the need for a quiet moment or two in most social occasions to replenish your energy levels, this is the chapter for you.

We are so desperate for self-sufficiency that we believe that we can become completely self-sufficient.

If we look more deeply, I believe that what scares us most about gatherings with friends is that the moment we leave and have a good time, we are bound to endless conversations and chatting for a certain amount of time. We want to make each moment of our lives productive. we block out any opportunity for excitement, spontaneity and joy, leading to our isolation even with a successful job or business.

We also know that there are very few locations where we are able to hide, be ourselves and be by ourselves even for a few minutes. This means that when we leave our home, we expose ourselves to a lot of conversations and to situations which require us to smile (even even though we think it ridiculous to make a smile on strangers) and to behave in spite of our wishes and to frequently meet strangers. Because of the probability of any of these happening once we have left our comfort zone for those who are introverts the decision to step out is a huge and unimaginable decision.

In addition, going out typically means interacting with random individuals to be part of a community because we can't remain at home at a gathering. In some cases introverts can be alone at an occasion. If, for instance, you were able to meet in person with a person you know or a group of friends and you want to retire from the world together.

Personally, my method every time I go out is to let myself be on my own and take part in the occasion. This means that I can allow myself to indulge in both my introverted as well as my extrovert side. Based on the circumstances I am often seen leaving conversations and dancing. If it's not a formal event, I usually sit for the time I have to sit and think about the whole occasion.

In my experience, since beginning the process, I've observed that monitoring people's reactions can be very enjoyable when you're outside of your comfortable zone. Additionally, there's a bit of appeal in this as other people think you are more attentive when they observe your interest in others' activities, but you are at your own choice.

It is important to note that certain people may be judging or annoyed that you finished your conversation only to go out dancing, which indicates your lack of interest in them. you really are. Others might consider your behavior rude and may even attempt to convey that you are not interested in them. But , really would you like to please them and then question your actions? I think so too. Please apologize if this makes you feel better but keep dancing.

In truth the people you encounter could be motivated by different motives like selfishness, superiority complex, envy etc. When you do your best to be respectful and avoid causing offence but you must remember that you've done not do anything wrong. Therefore, you should dispel any negative thoughts that come up and keep in the direction of replenishing your positive energy If this helps.

If you are sitting on your own during an occasion or gathering, you must be ready to answer questions like "What's going on?", "Has anything transpired?", "Are you exhausted?", "Are you doing well?", "You look tired".

At first, as I started this habit I soon became annoyed by these types of questions, as I usually responded with a hint of disdain: "Yes, I am exhausted" I would say. But once I had mastered the habit and encountered more often I realized that a lot of these people were trying to help others and the questions they asked were from a positive source.

If you are someone who is who are willing to adopt the habit of a lifetime, usually recommend giving them an honest response like "I am exhausted", "I need to take a rest for 5 to 10 minutes" or "I will be joining you shortly". Concise and polite, with no long explanation or lengthy story. This is clear evidence that you are planning to join them in five minutes, however for the moment you must be left to yourself.

The reality is that in order to be an open and fluid person your own unique style, you'll have to clear your emotional arteries, and break the links you've created between your social life and stress. It is never necessary to be a loser when trying to be social. You can effortlessly be an extremely fun person while not being an outgoing person. If you're in a situation and you need to take a break, do not be afraid or come up with an reason to justify the reason. Be truthful but direct. It doesn't mean you're a solitary sheep, rather it makes you more authentic to yourself. You might look similar to others However, you've decided to live your life in the light of your self-worth, and the majority of them might be scared to speak their truth.

Although the majority of people who attend occasions will be astonished and perhaps a little baffling to be by yourself during an event, some of them may find it distinctive being an independent person and do not have to be around other people to feel at ease.

Also being alone can provide an the opportunity for those who want to talk to you to talk without interrupting the conversation, or even dance along with another person. This is one benefit of this practice. If this kind of person approaches you, it's sensible to provide them with an open ear, even though you only had five minutes. It might or may not be a lasting friendship that is in the making. It's in your hands to decide whether you'd like to let the other side or prefer to be alone for this time. It's your choice.

We live in a world that associates sitting on your own as being insecure or unpopular which leads to people not engaging with you. These people are the mindset of the crowd and are addicts to approval. They will do anything to earn some sort of approval or recognition.

These aren't the type of people to look at when attending events. If you are individuals who are introverts Their actions or words may unintentionally harm you. The societal misunderstanding can be so depressing you could be pressured to constantly be part of the crowd, or any group, to keep conversations running, regardless of whether you like it or not.

In my personal and professional opinion, I'd like to encourage the urge to shed the societal norms and beliefs. If you are a person who is able to sit and observe others, it will not mean you are less popular than their peers. Don't be scared of fear of being judged by the fear of being viewed negatively by other people. Individuals are entitled to their own opinions in the same manner that you've decided to remain loyal to yourself and your own natural instincts regardless of the circumstance you're in.

Based on their cognitive capabilities and their basic human rights, they're at liberty to come to any conclusion they like. Why should they get together with such narrow-minded and blind people?

In the most depressing way is that your actions really mean that you've made the decision to go to the dance floor or just sit down and enjoy some time alone. It's as simple as that. There is no obligation to anyone any explanation.

Remember : You are self-sufficient.

Chapter 7: Become more confident in conversations

If you are more comfortable with how you are confident, the more easily the conversations you have. That's why it's essential to know how to build confidence in order to become a pro at small conversation.

How do you create this sense of confidence in the quickest way feasible? How can you go from a complete stranger to a hero in a matter of minutes? It could be easier more than you imagine.

Studies have shown that putting your best face can make you feel more comfortable when you start a conversation with anyone. If you can get your body to act more comfortably, you'll begin to feel as if you're doing it. Is that not logical? Here's a quick practice you can try to see if the theory is true for yourself.

Relax your eyes and slow the breathing process for few minutes.

Make sure you are in a good posture and stand straight.

Check that your muscles are in a relaxed state. Let as much tension go out of them as you are able.

Take a look around and see whether you experience any changes.

As I was doing this for myself, I was sure that I stood before the mirror and see whether I could detect the physical change. In the end I was pleasantly surprised to notice how calm and relaxed I appeared. I must admit that the exercise was short and helped me feel more confident than I did when I first began. If I altered my behavior I felt more different.

But your quest towards a more confident and self-confident you should not end there. You must build confidence in yourself to to talk with confidence and be successful in the world. Here are six effective tips to help you increase confidence.

You can turn off that inner voice which is always critiques you

Everybody has an inner voice within us. The voice that tells you that you're not attractive enough, or smart enough to stand out. I've had to fight this inner voice at times and has cost me lots of opportunities I was scared to accept. If you're constantly accepting your inner critic, you've got two options at this moment. Or, let it be the one to control you, or you can take a stand and block it out. If you allow it to control you, you'll never be able to get anywhere. But if you are able how to handle it right now, you'll be on the road towards getting to the level you've wanted be. It's all your choice.

Stop seeking perfection

You're likely to never be perfect and so working hard to attain perfection could be causing greater harm. If you strive to achieve perfection, you're giving yourself an environment of disappointment and pain. Most of the time it's you who hurt yourself the most. What's the most effective way to overcome this? Through cultivating a positive outlook throughout your life. Be grateful for what you can accomplish.

As long as you tried the best you could, view it a big accomplishment even if things didn't go as you imagined it would. Make sure you manage your expectations since reality can often contradict it. Be realistic and set achievable objectives instead of setting high standards for yourself.

Make a habit of reminding yourself each day of three aspects that will make you amazing.

If you're experiencing a feeling of being down in the bottom, one method to get yourself back on track is by recalling three factors that make you great. Record your responses in a notebook or on your smartphone so that you are able to keep a track of them that which you can refer to every now and again. In reliving your qualities or achievements that distinguish you You will be able to build an appreciation for your own. It also can be a fantastic mood boost.

Stop comparing yourself with other people.

Don't look to others for validation of your own. If you are in the habit of comparing yourself with other people, you become obsessed with what others have achieved, you leave no room for you. In reality, there always will be someone who is better than you. So , why should this alter your perception of yourself? In lieu of trying to measure yourself with other people, consider looking at the progress you've made in your own journey. It will certainly encourage you, but will aid you in taking the entire process one step at one time.

Don't be afraid of trying something different

When you push yourself to try something completely new, you're forcing yourself to step beyond your familiar zone. Not only will this give you satisfaction however, it gives you additional reasons to be grateful for yourself. It doesn't matter if you're chatting with the cute girl or guy in class, or talking up more to the boss you work for, you'll appreciate having that feeling of excitement every time you do something different to see if it's something you've never tried before. If things don't go as you'd like do not get too upset over it. It's important to remember that you attempted.

Maintain eye contact

It can be somewhat frightening to look at someone else's eyes but it can aid you tremendously to get your act in order. If you fail to look at someone it's not just a matter of losing the attention that the other person is talking with as well as your understanding of the scenario. It doesn't matter how intelligent or impressive you appear. If you don't keep eye contact it's not going convey your message with the individual you're speaking with.

When you've built up your confidence in yourself, it will be much easier to begin a conversation with almost everyone. When you're having a low moment at an occasion be aware that everything begins with yourself. You're the only person who is able to get through the conversation.

Chapter 8: The Little Talk Skills That Set you apart from other Humans

1. The ability to listen is in high demand.
Listening is a hand-off without question, one of the most difficult things to master. Why? because it takes a lot of effort, and the majority of people prefer simplicity over challenging tasks. So, because it's easier to express the things that are on your mind or to express your frustrations, or even how amazing you are, a lot of people prefer to talk than listen.

But, if you decide to be among those who really pay attention and are interested in people, you'll be a huge hit. You'll be surprised at the number of people who would like to keep chatting to you once they begin conversations. If the strangers around start to realize that you're one of the "aliens" who listen and are interested, you'll be surprised at how many people appreciate you and want to become your friends - and you might even be invited over to eat dinner.

Another reason that listening can be difficult for us is due to the multitude of distractions that tech-savvy have invented. Mark Zuckerberg, Bill Gates, Steve Jobs have created incredible little devices like Facebook, Computers, and iPhones which can be one of the largest distractions and annoyances of our time. Some people are actually addicted to their Smart Phone (http://www.webmd.com/balance/guide/addicted-your-smartphone-what-to-do).

The idea is that when you are engaged in conversations (especially when you are talking to someone who isn't familiar with you) it is crucial to switch off any distractions and focus on your ears and eyes. Also, you should trust your intuition.

* Challenge: For enjoyment, next time you start conversations, and start small talk, consider removing your use of the term "I" out of your vocabulary. I prefer this "I:You" ratio of 1:3. Do not talk about yourself in any way. Let your mind remain silent and be amazed and curious by the person right in the front of you. I love the idea of first asking an inquiry to satisfy curiosity, give a

brief response (not longer than 30 seconds to 1 minute) Then, you can ask another question to see if you're curious about the person who you've selected to talk to.

As I've previously mentioned it's important to put all of your past and future thoughts at the front of you before you enter an area. This allows you to remain in the present and let your mind wander rather than being anxious about the future or tense over the past. If this is a new concept to the you or haven't yet mastered it then take a look at my Bestseller How to Be Present in the Moment. The book contains six steps that will teach you how you can easily be in the present.

One of the most valuable things we can offer other people is our ears eyes, and our hearts for listening. We can be able to show that we truly care and acknowledge the amazing human being who is in front of us. It is possible to see how fast people be drawn to your presence, simply by being attentive and being understanding.

2. A little slow, but and not too slow. Just in the middle.

Speedy talk can make the listener feel overwhelmed. You might even notice that your listener was unable to comprehend the words you spoke of because of your ability to "rap" the words you're speaking. Additionally, it could make it appear as if you're frightened and uneasy of what you're discussing.

If you speak at a slow pace, it could cause the listener to become bored, and they may be able to fall asleep and start thinking about how wonderful it would be to lay in bed and sleep out. However you could notice people listening to you become distracted and wandering at the wall or at his watch , as if anxious and eager to find out who else is around.

It varies between listeners however the most effective way to deal with it is to begin at an appropriate pace so that the person listening can hear and understand your speech and not get bored. Once you have an understanding of the voice of the other person you should follow their pace.

Do it for a few minutes of time, and then a feeling of mutual trust will be created. Also, matching the audio speeds creates a more rapid and stronger connection and gives you a feeling of confidence.

3. Use your enthusiasm and make use of tones.

The monotone sound is dull. Have you ever been in a class in which you were required to sit through an insipid (boring) lecture from the teacher each class, and it required all of your energy to remain awake? Even though the teacher might be Einstein smart, the instructor was unable to draw audience in because of the lack of passion about the topic.

While the speaker might be knowledgeable and passionate about the topic however, if what's going on inside isn't reflected in the public, the audience aren't going to be entertained. If someone brings an intense level of enthusiasm and excitement to a subject being discussed, it creates the audience to a variety of colours the words spoken by someone else than being merely monochrome text. This doesn't mean that you have to be completely enthusiastic all the time, but just sprinkle a bit of excitement throughout your story to keep viewers engaged. If you're looking for the details of how to become enthusiastic or to transform every "boring" tale into one that is an "amazing and memorable" one check out The Storytelling Method.

The emotions are like the colors, and black and white are the two words. People are drawn to emotion because it is the essence of life. If you are able to trigger an emotional response, the topic you're discussing can be remembered by the people who listen to your talk.

Passion inspires enthusiasm, and that is the reason it's important to discuss something that you're passionate about and if you're not passionate about the subject , try to you should find something you are passionate about when you speak. Focus on it since we frequently require reminders of our goals to keep us motivated. If, for instance, you're teaching a class about theater arts and come across the topic of Shakespeare (which you hate because of its peculiar word structure) but you love the feather hats or more characters in the play consider using that feather to remind you of something that brings you a smile. Perhaps you are a fan of that name "Puck" which was one of the major characters from Shakespeare's "A Midsummer Night's Dream" So you'll keep the hockey puck in your possession or write that name onto a sheet paper beside you, and each time you look at it, you'll be smiling. It could be funny, odd or bizarre initially, but you'll begin to realize how enjoyable, exciting and useful this technique can be.

Another way to generate enthusiasm is to frame the idea, and then attach it to something you love - but not just enjoy, but also love! Something that you have a strong desire for as passion generates excitement, and enthusiasm creates excitement, which in turn makes for more attentive listeners. Look at the issue from a different angle and the larger image to see who or what else, is out there. For instance, perhaps you're not enthusiastic about traveling to new places or getting to know new people, but you are passionate about and are driven to assist others, which helps you stay motivated.

Maybe you're not too enthusiastic about discussing roller coasters however your mom (who you adore) has a passion for roller coasters. To increase the excitement, you could imagine how thrilled you mom will be riding the roller coaster, holding her hands in the air wavering a peace sign from above, or in the back of your image flipping over you the bird, adding humor and excitement to your image. When you do this, you'll be able to notice changes in the tone of your voice when you tell your story.

Begin with enthusiasm and begin by adding the tone of your voice up and down in your speech. It's as if you are on an infant rollercoaster. From the comfort at home, you could pretend to be an singer or actor in preparation for a show. You can practice your voice using "voice muscles" to broaden vocal range. Here is a video for opening you're voice: https://www.youtube.com/watch?v=Q5hS7eukUbQ

Overall, enthusiasm is appealing, and can attract listeners. If you wish to be noticed and remembered, you must be enthusiastic. There are plenty of more examples at: https://www.youtube.com/results?search_query=how+to+sound+enthusiastic

4. Pronoun-ci-ate Your Words

Do not confuse yourself. It is not fun for people to have to say "What?" or "I'm sorry, can you repeat this?" or "Pardon?" or "Huh?" You get the idea. If the person listening has to repeat the phrase several times they may start to feel a little frustrated and thoughts may race across the listener's head wondering if something is wrong their hearing, or whether they should have their hearing tested, but it's actually the case that the speaker is mumbling. Thus, you should pronounce your words in a way that every syllable sounds perfectly distinct. If you are constantly hearing "huh?" then it is time to rethink, "e-nun-ci-ate" because you are speaking in a mumble.

Being in an area crowded with people is a sign that there are eye-rolling at you and judging you on your appearance. There will be ears looking at you, ready to judge your speech and tone of voice speed, and accent (all of which can affect your voice's pronunciation) regardless of whether you want the way they pronounce it. Make sure you can pronounce each word, especially when you speak with an accent. It isn't a good idea to let someone think that you've said "Where's the lavatory?" when you really wanted to say "Where's that juice?" Or thinking you were saying "french Flies" but you actually intended to say "french fries."

The next section I'll explain how to pronounce your voice to ensure that you have your voice the way you'd like, and increase your confidence when talking to strangers.

5. Make sure to increase (or lower) to increase or decrease.

I'm not sexist to any extent. However, from my own experiences in beginning thousands of small talk conversations, I've observed that males who speak slightly more booming voice than the other group when they start a conversation, it will make him more popular. If he uses an unresonant voice, he's likely to not even be heard or noticed even if he's tallor stunningly handsome due to the fact that his presence isn't powerful enough. There's nothing that draws people to listen.

Females on the other hand, is considered more acceptable if they speak with a soft voice than those around them in the beginning, because the presence of a woman is more noticeable in comparison to a male's. Men by nature are aware of this and women tend to be more tolerant of women who are in an exchange than men. If she starts small talk in a louder tone it is usually viewed as a domineering persona, and is less popular (especially by women around her).

6. Make sure you use words you can understand.

If you're not sure of the meaning behind a term, don't use the word. It's simple. If you use something in order to appear smart, but you don't comprehend the meaning or the best way to utilize it, it can cause a backlash. People can be distracted from what you're talking about and then get stuck asking, "Why did she use this word? Does she even have any idea what the word signifies? Or do I have to "Google" the meaning of the word since I'm certain it's a reference to something different." It is easy for the listener remain attentive, focused and use words you already know.

If you don't understand the meaning behind a term avoid using it. keep it in your head as well as "Google" the meaning of the word following the discussion.

Returning to the primary issue voice. If you aren't happy regarding your voice it's your responsibility to do something to change it. It is possible to hire the services of a voice coach or therapy, or if you are looking to save money then you can fix your voice by yourself. This is a technique that has been successful for many including myself.

1. Record your voice
2. Take note of it and make a note of the things you would like to alter.
3. Record your voice again
4. Remind yourself, and then keep track of what you'd like to alter.
5. Stop for a rest.
6. Repeat the process for 30 mins in the morning and for 30 minutes at night, for 30 days.
7. Take a look back over the course of a month to look at the remarkable improvement you've achieved. If it's still not the way you'd like it to be keep working until you're there.

It will be apparent that you're making changes in how people react to you, and you'll feel more confident when you meet with strangers to talk.

Chapter 9: Tips On Influencing People

We all have to influence others, but don't have the necessary knowledge about how to do doing it. When at work, or any other place you are with people, we feel the need of building trust and establishing relationships based on our influence over people instead of manipulating them. Anyone can be a leader, however it can be difficult to master, particularly when it comes to gaining people's feel respected and think of your leadership qualities. Being a leader is an act of influence over people and building confidence. You've probably experienced situations in which a person has great abilities and has the capability of giving the best but is unable to climb to the level they desire as their competitors are elected by large numbers. This is usually an effect of influence in the event that certain individuals have the ability to influence other individuals more than others.

Influence is the ability to influence individuals' actions, thoughts or opinions and make decisions. By definition it sounds impossible. This is why you might think how someone could get into your brain and alter the way you think. It is possibleand many great leaders use the technique of influencing others to win their trust, respect and also the authority they enjoy. In essence, influence is conformity. It is the act of making someone perform what you want them to do.

Influence can be found everywhere It is possible to use the opportunity to meet new people or collaborate with people without authority. Influence is an important factor for individuals to accomplish their goals motivations, goals, and ideas and ensure that they are always in their corner. Control without manipulation can be quite difficult and is a process that is usually measured consistent, predictable, and repeated. The two, influence and manipulation have significant distinctions despite both relying on the mind to alter individuals' mental habits.

Types of Influence

Negative Influence

This is the exact opposite of positive influence and is usually is the most harmful type of influence, as the people who use this type of influence tend to be focused on the power or authority of others only. This means that they are self-centered and proud and, typically employ force or some other form of trickery to rise to the highest levels. They are leaders but they are not respected and people are unable to follow them and to listen to them. The title says it all their results are usually negative, affecting either the group or organization in a negative way. These leaders, even more don't attain any goal that is beneficial as their results are usually insufficient. It is imperative to take not follow or avoid them because their motivation to lead is generally detrimental.

Neutral Influence

Neutral influences are generally accepted practices and beliefs of a leader that have neither any negative or positive effect on the other members of the group. They generally neutral and have little negative impact, which is what makes them different from others. They don't contribute nor subtract value to an organization or team. They don't offer any assistance and don't take any steps or are proactive in any manner. Although they do not have any benefits or disadvantages, these leaders tend to sit back and wait for the team or their subordinates under their direction to move forward and meet their objectives as they don't have any influence. Another type that you ought to stay clear of because these leaders do no means to improve their positions.

Positive Influence

Leaders are a great example of positive influence because they contribute value to their team and keep them in a positive way. This form of influence that can be very effective particularly for leaders who are active in their interactions with people and exhibit positive attitudes and behaviors towards other people. The benefit of this kind of influence is that the leader is one who develops and builds relationships with others by inspiring as well as leadership and instructing others. Being a positive influencer means that you will quickly establish yourself as an instructor and assist others to succeed. Additionally, this kind of influence requires higher standards of commitment, dedication and a desire to ensure that everyone succeeds in life.

Life-Changing Influence

The most respected and highest kind of influence, and it is comprised of some people who are able to get to this point. While they may be an influencer with positive qualities being in this class, becoming one of leaders can take many years or even decades to develop the strategies to lead well and transform lives. Contrary to positive influence influence is the ability to make choices that will forever alter the lives of individuals by words or actions. The people you influence stay in the same position even after the leader has long absent from an organization or group. Leaders who have a positive impact usually invest all of their lives their time and energy to help others succeed without pride, greed or the desire to satisfy their own needs. Influencers who have a life-changing impact are Oprah Winfrey, Mother Teresa along with Abraham Lincoln.

How to influence people

Establish Relations

Being a leader starts with building strong relationships with your fellow leaders and especially when you are looking to make new acquaintances. One method to establish a strong relationship is to have an outgoing and friendly personality which can be a major influence on people around you when they feel attractive and comfortable. Engage with others and without prejudice to create an impression by addressing people by their name in order to make your message more personal. Engage in discussions frequently, which builds your confidence, but don't force opinions, but rather connecting them to the subject in the present. Talk about your experiences when discussing other people's concerns, and remembering to listen to different viewpoints.

Create Positive Reputations

A key aspect to influence people is creating a reputation that is distinct from the crowd. This can be accomplished by constantly admitting that you made mistakes when you're not right as well as pointing out mistakes of others in an intelligent positive, indirect and constructive way. In addition, demonstrate your knowledge in areas that require an extensive understanding of while performing things that will make people appreciate and admire your way of life. You can also build your name by showing a desire to study by observing with an open mind from your teachers or from errors made in the process.

Help Others

In terms of influence, many focus on their peers, an additional method to win the trust of people is to offer help in various ways. For instance, you can approach people with a more friendly manner. Don't be a jerk or pushy because this can show signs of pride and desire for the power of other people. Be a good friend by showing empathy with regards to your the beliefs of others and their actions which must be only positive. Make positive changes in the society and avoid giving commands or orders, which are generally considered to be unprofessional. Be sure to spare those who feel ashamed by embracing people who offer ideas and fixing them and letting the ideas be their own. Finally, be kind to others , not becoming jealous. Allow them to feel inspired by your generosity, but do not praise just for the sake that it makes them feel better.

Analyzing Communication Styles

Understanding communication styles is a crucial aspect particularly when it comes to leaders figuring out how they interact with their colleagues. Furthermore, it allows people to comprehend how they interact with their friends family and colleagues and implement the changes needed to be more active and confident interaction. This is especially important for those who influence other people; they have the opportunity to communicate and express their thoughts. There are different kinds of communication styles that can employ several methods when speaking in various scenarios.

Assertive Style

It is the most efficient method of communication that is typically employed by those with more self-confidence. It is the most healthiest and incorporates all positive qualities of communication which include behavioural verbal, language and nonverbal methods. The behavioral traits typically involve accepting compliments as well as being accountable to your conduct, observing your own rules, being respectful of the opinions of others as well as sharing opinions, as well as emotionally. The language used in this manner is calm and uses non-verbal behaviors such as uninhibited, open and symmetrical posture expressions, facial expressions, gestures and a moderately pitched voice.

Agressive Style

An aggressive style of communication is one that employs a threatening and ineffective tone of voice towards other people. Contrary to an assertive tone an aggressive person typically employs a loud voice, eyes that glare or make scowling expressions. They are swift and quick. They also make use of postures to make them appear than others. They're more aggressive, intimidating, defensive aggressive, demanding, and intimidating. They are people who have negative influence. They often display confidence and arrogance when in the position of authority. A threatening manner of communication generally makes the recipient feel frightened, humiliated and disdainful during the exchange.

Passive Style

It is sometimes described as passive-aggressive since those who practice these types appear like they are normal on the outside, but they are bitter inside. People who use the passive style of communication are more likely to employ different ways to express their anger than using violence or aggression. People who do this feel defeated and angry and can end up harming themselves through the process. Communication behaviours tend to be not reliable, sarcastic or even patronising and can be characterized as indirect aggression. The nonverbal behavior includes the soft and sweet voice as well as asymmetrical postures. that quick and jerky style.

Submissive Style

People who are submissive include people who only want to please other people to avoid conflict despite any difficulties they might encounter during the process. This kind of behavior makes others feel valued and has more authoritative over someone who is submissive. The most common behavioural patterns displayed by these individuals are apologizing, opting-out of confrontations, remaining silent and constantly feeling like being a victim.

Nonverbal behavior includes fidgeting, twisting gestures, soft voice and a absence of eye contact while still looking down and being a bit small in the face of encounters. The people who are on the receiving end typically feel angry, beneficial or guilty. They may also feel angry and resentful.

Manipulative Style

While not the most appropriate method of communication for everyone, manipulative individuals tend to be more sophisticated and clever. This kind of communication could effectively influence others, particularly people who are feeling lost. People who feel lost often appear to be superior, and if you push yourself to the top you become more calculating and continue to be dominant in positions of leadership. The language they use usually conceals the intention behind it and the person who is receiving it be unaware of the message being portrayed. In this way, manipulative individuals tend to become shrewd and ask for things in indirect ways as well as sulking. They can also manipulate others, and cause people to feel guilt. The voice that is used in this type of communication is typically smug, condescending and envious, with sad and pathetic expressions.

Benefits of Understanding the Styles of communication to influence people

As an influential leader who leads others by example, knowing the various kinds of communication styles put you in the frontline to be able to manage different groups under your direction. There are people who exhibit more than one type of communication, based on the circumstances. Understanding how they behave and behave in these scenarios also helps you to deal with them in a positive manner. As as a leader, you're allowed to employ any type of communication however it should be respectful, rational and beneficial for you and your team members or organization. Knowing about various communication styles in the future will allow you to be an effective leader in difficult situations.

Certain words and phrases that affect people

The English language has five of the most convincing words that have been proven to motivate people to participate in actions that influencers expect from them. There are also words that are used in various areas such as business in order to make customers more likely to purchase the product they are interested in. They are not just helpful in convincing people, but are they also aid in keeping top positions for influential people. The most effective words that are used are

And

"And" is a popular expression used for influencing people specifically when focusing on particular product or information. For example, 'you've spent a long time in this book, and there's still a lot to discover.' This implies that regardless of how far a reader has enjoyed and absorbed the book, there's plenty to learn. In this way, it creates an impact that when you read you're likely to investigate more that you would never have imagined. When you influence others, it can cause a reader the desire to read more and alter the way they think or thought process and his or her own opinions.

Because

It is a different type of work that provides a more detailed clarification of what the details or products are about. "Because," can be used to present two scenarios in the form of a statement that indicate an understanding of the person who is receiving. For instance, "the grass is extremely green because it rained the previous week.' In this instance, the word 'because is used to explain the reasoning that you simply say "the grass is very clean today.' This phrase, therefore, attempts to provide an effective capability for a person to comprehend the significance of an event.

You

When you use the term "you" in reference to personal experiences, it is easy to dissociate your personal expertise from the expertise of your reader or your audience. While some may also employ the word 'I' to convey authority in their work, both are likely to have the same purpose. But, 'you' tries to communicate and engage effectively, especially when it comes to influencing an even larger audience there. In some instances using the word 'I' makes the impression that you're insecure and uneasy about sharing your experience with other people. For instance, 'as you read this article, you'll discover different communication styles', and "while I read this, I will be learning about different methods of communicating.' The first and the second examples drive home the point. When it comes to convincing those around you, this one has more impact than the other.

Guarantee

To influence those working in the business world You must make use of more appealing and attractive terms. One of them words is 'guarantee'. It attempts to define product quality and long-lasting. The reason for this is that the marketplace is rife with fraud, and the only way to ensure the sale of products is by providing promises to customers. In this instance the word 'guarantee is employed to convince customers into buying a particular product based on the authenticity of the product. But, the business world is filled with other terms used to persuade consumers to purchase, which include phrases like discounts, free exclusive, limited, and.

What Does That Mean?

The expression "which means" can also be a significant influencer on people, thereby changing the way they view certain thoughts and ideas. Although it sounds like a typical phrase within language, it is not. English spoken language, the phrase is an important message that can inspire people to engage in a different action. In addition, it could be used to provide a thorough description of what an act or behavior is about, based on the way you apply them. For instance, "you've attended this course for a certain duration, which indicates that you're learning something that will add importance to your daily life.'

Methods of Speaking to Persuade, and influence

Appealing to the public

Influencers typically recognize the importance of their audiences and make use of opportunities to engage with them by placing them first in conversations. In this scenario this method, you must put your audience in the spotlight and ensuring they know about and following the discussion. To influence your audience The first strategy to employ is to make sure that they are at the front when highlighting your key points. This means that you should employ the most effective method of communication, making your speech engaging and informative. Affecting your audience with your message gives greater chances of understanding and involvement in the discussion.

The use to Nonverbal Communication Skills

A few people have an organized, well-organized and plausible speech which will leave your audience happy with the topic. If you can accompany your speech with non-verbal signals, you are more likely to get your listeners engaged and focused. A few of the characteristics of nonverbal components are general appearance, emotions expressions, gestures and facial expressions. Utilizing both nonverbal and verbal components will not only help to convey the message but also makes sure that the message is effective and is delivered in a more rational way. The combination of both will significantly influence the attention of more people in a single glance.

Utilization of actionable examples

There are some topics that require some clarification due to their complexity, or else appear impossible. Therefore, the audience might lose interest or perceive the presentation as an impossible topic with only limited factors. In this scenario the best approach to make the presentation more useful is through the use of concrete examples. These should be multiple. Furthermore, you may decide to use your audience as examples, since they will be the main audience for your presentation. Examples could also incorporate personal stories, experiments, or images that are displayed on your slides.

Make sure to emphasize critical cases

In spite of using both nonverbal and verbal components and examples, there are people who might not be able to focus through the entire presentation and be able to comprehend all the information. The most effective method to employ in this situation is to highlight those crucial points in the sentence. This can be accomplished by putting a pause at any time you feel the topic is vital; you can employ phrases like "listen carefully" to emphasize the statement and to change the tone and volume for these parts. It is also possible to move more in proximity to the listener, and maintain eyes on them when focusing on crucial points of your speech.

Participate the audience

In order to effectively influence people to influence people, it is important to allow them to participate in the discussion in question. There are some who remain calm throughout the entire speech, not ever asking or adding any additional information to the subject. If this happens you might not be able to influence them, particularly when you are unable to engage them to the discussion. This can be accomplished by putting out a call to act to get the audience's feedback, then entice them with the ideas for coming in, then then plan an intimate meeting to express their thoughts on the presentation. This method has been utilized by a variety of leaders to engage the audience and earned an impressive reputation with the public. This technique allows you to build your credibility that earned confidence from those you would like to influence.

Chapter 10: Creating Confidence in Small Conversations

Some people find that small talk can be a relaxing and pleasant experience. Some people are irritated and grumpy which is why they try to avoid it at all costs. It's good to know that people who find even small talk stressful could learn to master it through practice. If you're in that situation, increasing confidence levels can help greatly. If you're confident at a high levels, it will be much easier to talk to people and have small conversations.

You are able to confidently introduce yourself to people in different situations, be it with people in an elevator or hallway and waiting to see an occasion begin. If you're working in the field of business or plan to develop your career, then doing your small talk confidently can benefit you. It can let people who are around you know about your and your abilities, or help improve your professional relationships. You can also leverage confidence and your skills in small-talk to build your network.

For helping you build your confidence level, or look more confident when engaging in small conversations and keeping the conversation flowing This section will provide some helpful suggestions.

Slowly speak

Many people have the ability to talk fast in times of stress. Other people are naturally fast talkers. Whatever the reason, whether you are doing it intentionally or unconsciously, talking too fast could indicate that you are not confident or lack authority. Additionally there's an increased chance you'll make mistakes particularly when speaking certain words. This can also limit the amount of time you have to be aware of the words you speak from your mouth.

If you're looking to convey confidence in small discussions Try speaking in a slow manner. Allow your words to flow. Be sure your sentences are grammatically correct and have a rhythm. Slower and more coherent speech will allow your audience time to absorb the meaning of what you're speaking. It also helps you avoid making critical errors that could affect the credibility of your communication.

Make use of to pause

Another method to display your confidence while speaking slowly while still being confident is to employ pauses in a strategic manner. It is possible to pause in a creative way each time to make what that you're speaking more powerful. If you're able, make sure to do this during the most important portion of your speech. It gives weight to the topic you're discussing as well as allowing the person you're talking to for them to comprehend it.

The great thing about the pauses is that they provide you with the chance to think about your ideas while making plans for the things you'll be saying in the following. If you're just beginning to learn about small-sized conversations, then this is helpful since it makes your appearance more confident while giving your expertise and authority. This will make it easier to connect with people who are around you.

Get your posture back in order

In addition to the words that leave your mouth, your body language is equally important. If, for instance, you are standing or sitting in the presence of someone, it is important to improve your posture. Maintain a straight and upright posture, by putting your arms back. It is also recommended to keep your head up. You'll appear more confident by doing this, and it can aid in gaining the confidence to speak to anyone.

In addition, correcting your posture prior to beginning an informal conversation, and making sure that you maintain it will also allow you to move your body. This gives you the opportunity to breathe and talk with greater efficiency. Because posture is a work-intensive process and practice, it's essential to do it frequently. Over time, you'll be accustomed to it. You'll notice that you're slouching, and rectify it immediately.

Smile

If you'd like the little conversations you started to end in a positive way, make your goal to smile. You should ensure that people who are around you feel like you're someone they could meet. Display your warm and friendly aspect to them, and you'll have a better transition from the casual conversation to more interesting and deep conversations. If you're new to the business of starting small conversations, don't be afraid of being uncomfortable in doing this. Sooner or later, you'll master your art of smiling properly and displaying your friendly and friendly character.

It's also recommended that you practice smiling so that you can smile in a professional manner without appearing like a creep. One suggestion is to practice your smile before the mirror. All you need to do is sit in front of the mirror. Close your eyes, then gaze down. The next step is to look up and smile. Close your eyes as you do so. If you see your real smile when you look in the mirror, then that is the one you need to practice. This is what you need to show your friend you're chatting with.

Eliminate all unneeded thoughts

These thoughts and worries might be the ones keeping you from talking with someone, or appearing confident when you approach him. Be aware the fact that your thoughts may be just within your mind. They aren't real. Actually, they're quite different from the reality. If, for instance, you think you're not at home when you're in a certain situation, take note that it's not only you that feels it.

People around you might be feeling the same. Be aware that everyone has some insecurities of their own. The person sitting next to you at an event might have wanted to chat with you and you can be comfortable and avoid feeling uncomfortable. However, you should be careful not to overthink it.

If you see someone you want to get to know do not wait over three seconds to get in touch with the person. If you allow that time to be in between you and him, you'll simply end up analyzing the situation, which makes it more difficult to start the conversation. Begin by introducing yourself immediately, so that you'll instantly be from that uncomfortable and uncomfortable situation. If you receive an affirmative response, your stress and anxiety will soon be replaced by cooler and more calm you.

Don't give in to the stress or anxiety. Be careful not to overthink things and you'll certainly be able to tackle any attempts to start small conversations easily and confidently.

Chapter 11: Learn how to talk about yourself in a respectful manner

There's something more unpleasant than speaking with someone who spends most of their time boasting about themselves. People like this frequently talk for hours on their kids or the trials and tribulations of their work as well as relationships with the spouse and how wonderful it is, and also about their money. They can be described as shrewd (to say the least) and you shouldn't try to become one of these kinds of people. They are viewed as a nuisance and you're unlikely to create an excellent impression when you're constantly boasting while making people whom you're chatting feel less than. With this kind of information regarding the person you don't wish to be The question is what should you do in a way to make sure that you appear comfortable and discreet? That's the topic this chapter is about.

Twenty Second Rule Twenty Second Rule

In the event that you are reading this article, chances are you're an individual who doesn't like talking a lot. If this describes you, it's likely that you're following the rule of twenty seconds without even knowing that it exists. There have been studies that show that in small-talk individuals do not like being engaged for longer then twenty minutes at stretch. In between 20 and 30 minutes of conversation can lead to a feeling of the feeling of being liked and a sense of agreeability, it is after that, the person talking is likely to be seen as being too tense to the person in question. If you're the type of person who likes to talk in a rambling manner when you're stressed This is definitely something you'll need to improve. The fact in the matter is, in an environment of brief conversation, the amount of time you speak is crucial. If you've been blabbering for longer than forty seconds, you stand a lower chance likelihood of being viewed positively by the person who is listening to your remarks.

Embody Curious George

This strategy is a reference to the previous chapter , which focused on the issue of being present. However, it is applicable to this chapter too. If you're engaged in small conversations it is important to make sure you're genuinely interested in the person you're talking to even if you have to pretend for a few minutes. Consider it this way. Do you think you would be more than happy to speak with someone who seemed uninterested and didn't engage with you? You can influence a person's perception of worth by asking them questions that are thoughtful throughout the conversation because it will show that you value your thoughts, points of view, and viewpoint regarding a specific subject.

Get advice from a professional

Instead of talking to someone about yourself, a different option is to solicit advice. This is a difficult method to employ, due to reasons of convenience. You do not want the topic of your advice to be too intruding or a burden. So long as you remember this the idea of asking for advice is an excellent method to keep the conversation moving. It's also a well-known fact that people generally like to tell stories about themselves based upon their own experiences. If you seek suggestions from someone, you're giving them the right to share their own personal stories, but without coming across as self-centered or uninvolved. This approach will probably alleviate some of the burden off you since the person with whom you're talking won't think about yourself, but more about the story they're telling.

Do not allow yourself to be enticed to talk About Your Most Favorite Subject

In the same vein of following the rule of twenty-seconds it is recommended to not discuss your favourite subject when you can. As an example, we've most likely met someone who has recently acquired a new pet or experienced a new grandchild. If you begin to ask those people about their new pet or the baby that has entered their lives, you're likely to be involved in a conversation that lasts at least 20 minutes or longer (if you're lucky). Don't let this happen to you. If you're enthusiastic about a particular subject, it's best to save the topic for your buddies as you are aware you can count on them to either tolerate the things you say or beg you to stop after you've beaten the subject to the point of exhaustion. If you're certain that you're able to rein yourself in and limit the conversation about this subject to a minimum, good for you. but when you're just trying to engage in conversation Your most talked about topics should be reserved for people who already know you more than those who aren't sure about who you really are.

The Why is the focus and the How.

Finally, if you're playing curious George when you're asking lot of questions to someone who you don't know well, you should concentrate on asking questions that begin at "Why" or "How" rather than is, Who, or when. What is the reason and how are two ones that require some explanation. What Questions, Who and When are those that are able to be explained with one or two words. When you ask these kinds of questions, you will be in a position to take some the burden off of you as the focus will be on what the other person has to say and will prevent the need to talk for at the very least some minutes.

With all the methods discussed throughout this article, it's crucial to keep in mind that people love to talk about themselves. When you can get someone engaged in a particular issue that's particularly appealing to them and you've opened the doors where the dialogue can become mostly about the other party and not so much about you. Self-consciousness isn't something you should avoid when you engage in small talk, so long as you've got the right tools available to allow the conversation to focus more on the other person and less about you.

Chapter 12: Understanding and How to Deal With Different Kinds of Conversationalists

You will meet a variety of people when you talk. It's possible to enjoy a chat with a few of them, however there are others who could place him in a difficult situation. This chapter have discussed certain conversationalists that you could come across and the ways you can manage these.

The Best Conversationalists

Here are some examples of conversationalists you'd like to emulate If you wish to be the talk of the town. You can also learn how to talk to one should you be in their group.

The Artist Conversationalist

This is the person everyone hopes to be. He is the person who is able to be able to hold the conversation for all. He has the ability to draw remarks or a response from other participants. He is a person who is able get people talking during conversations. He is typically the person who initiates the conversation.

If you come across this kind of situation of situation, be prepared to express your opinions or make statements during the conversation. The artist conversationalist is there to assist you. Also, you should get help from the artist's conversationalist.

There are certain things to avoid when dealing with an artist or a professional. Here are a few of them:

Don't try to outdo him. The artist is often in the spotlight. If you attempt to take his attention some of the people in the group might think you're desperate to be noticed. Some may suggest to leave instead. Even worse, some might force you to allow the conversationalist artist talk to you.

Don't make your position clear. If you're in agreement with the conversationalist artist simply nod your head. Don't tell the person that you agree with him or that's good except when it is absolutely necessary. You could end up looking like a snob or cheerleader during the conversation.

Don't try to outdo him, but don't lose your character Also.

The Intelligent Conversationalist

This is the person who is knowledgeable of a variety of topics. He always begins as the listener. He doesn't present any issues, but instead provides some information or comments that could make the conversation more lively. Sometimes, however, the intelligent conversationalist can also create awkward moments in conversations because of his high-level of intellectual response.

To be able to have a great conversation with a smart conversationalist it is essential to keep a library on the general knowledge about current events, as well as other subjects that you encounter every day. It is also important to quickly break the ice in awkward times. One method to do this is to seek clarification from the conversationalist who is smart. However, you must be aware of how you pose the questions.

Clarification questions like "What did you said?" "Huh? Do you want to repeat it?" and "Eh?" is a sign of disrespect during the course of a conversation. Instead, you could reiterate what was said and clarify what the speaker was trying to convey in it.

For example, John stated, "Long ago, Varicella was difficult to treat."

The wrong way to answer: "Eh? Varicella What?"

The best way to ask: "Varicella was difficult to treat? How do I define Varicella?"

If you ask it in the right method, you don't appear to be ignorant of the subject or plain dumb. Instead, you appear as someone with an interest in this subject.

The Subtle Conversationalist

The subtle conversationalist is nearly identical to the intelligent conversationalist. The only distinction in subtle one can only speak when spoken as well. In contrast to the smart conversationalist, the latter does not express his own view or opinion. He is the best person to listen to the group.

A subdued conversationalist usually joins discussions in groups only in the role of an observer. To get him to actively participate, you must inquire about his views on the subject.

But, you need to be aware of how you can bring the conversationalist to join in the conversation. Continuously provoking the subtle conversationalist's hand to talk can cause them to feel a bit irritated.

The Bad Conversationalists

Below are the boring parts in the discussion. They are the ones who cause the conversation to become boring. Avoid being one of them.

1. The "Clever-Bore" Conversationalist

"Clever-Bore" is a term used to describe a "Clever-Bore" conversationalist can describe themselves as an individual who claims to be a conversationalist with a lot of knowledge however, they only engage with topics that are simple to all. They usually focus the topic or fact that they already knows.

A good example of "clever-bore "clever-bore" is someone who will fervently discuss the ways identical twins form during a discussion with the doctor and claim that they are the only person who is aware of it.

The term "clever bore" is a difficult person to talk to. They could end up destroying the conversation immediately or cause half the group to leave.

To confront an "clever-bore" You should refrain from confronting him. Be sure to not mention that you or the entire group know the specifics that he's trying to show. Instead, you can add some information about the subject to add interest.

For instance: Peter claimed, "Identical twins are formed from the same zygote. A daughter cell split from the rest of the cells during mitosis , and then developed into a separate zygote." This fact is well-known to doctors as well as to the general public.

To spice up the concept laid out by Peter you can add some information that might not be available to the other members of the group.

In the previous example you could add a remarks like "But did you know the article that a group of identical twins with different genders? I didn't know there was a possibility for twins' chromosomes to alter and alter the sex of the different twin to shift."

The topic discussed is different from Peter's, other doctors of the group are able to provide their opinions on the topic. However, ensure that the addition you make should enhance the contributions of others in the discussion and limit the amount of input"clever bore "clever bore" could bring to the conversation.

2. The Apathetic Conversationalist

The apathetic conversationalist can be described similar to the gentle conversationalist. Similar to the subtle conversationalist the apathetic conversationalist begins as a participant in the group. But, unlike the subtle conversationalist, the apathetic one is easily bored by artistic or intelligent conversations. He is also not able to cover his disinterest in the subject. He might occasionally sigh, yawn or sigh when someone is speaking.

An effective approach to confront the conversationalist who is apathetic in the event that you are the speaker is to shift the spotlight to the depressed conversationalist. He can start by introducing with a topic that might appeal to him. This could lead to two results.

In the beginning, the nonchalant person in the conversation could make the conversation go on for longer by introducing topics that is interesting to him.

In addition, it could place him in a corner or force him to end the discussion.

3. "Broken Record "Broken-Record" Conversationalist

"Broken-Record" conversationalists "broken-record" conversalist who speaks about the same topics or repeats the same stories in the course of a conversation. They will talk about the same stories so frequently that other people might have memorized. They are people who freeze the conversation since they don't wish to repeat the same remarks they have previously made.

If you are in a situation it is not a good idea to mention that you have had heard about the incident before. According to psychologists, anyone who talks about something over and over is seeking a judgement.

The best approach to address"broken-record "broken-record" should be to offer the person the recognition they desire and then change the subject or direct the conversation to a different person involved in the conversation.

4. "Excessive "Life-sharer" Conversationalist

The "life-sharer" chatteralist is someone who will only talk about his life experiences and how he came to this kind of life. It can be an intriguing and inspirational subject. However, it could turn into an uninteresting conversation, especially when the sharing of life is excessive or is more about boasting than sharing.

If the conversationalist discusses the way he purchased an Ferrari this would be a fascinating subject. However, if he speaks about the number of Ferraris the owner has and the intends to purchase 2 more Ferraris, he might just want to showcase.

If someone else shares their life experiences, you must recognize the positive aspects that he has lived. However, if he decides to talk about his life in the course of a conversation, you could easily change the subject or direct the conversation to someone else who shares similar interests or previously been in the same position similar to the person who spoke before.

5. The "Pitiful" Conversationalist

A pathetic conversationalist is someone who talks only about his issues or struggles. He's like a broken-record conversationalist and a life-sharer together, however, it is only about sad and savage stories. He doesn't just make the conversation painful, but also creates a boring conversation.

If you have to deal with a pathetic chatterbox, you must congratulate the guy for persevering through his troubles and remind him that it is something worth being celebrated. In this way, the topic are able to easily change from a sad to a joyful one.

If a member of the group experienced similar issues once as well, you may request that person to give his thoughts on the pathetic conversationalist , and then use that to switch the conversation.

6. "Monologuist" or the "Monologuist" also known as Egoistic Conversationalist

The monologuist is determined to be the one who talks. He would like to be the expert and the focus in the dialogue.

They find it easy to be offended when they are interrupted, or when they are unable to stay within their comfortable zone. They usually feel nervous and afraid to get caught up in topics that they aren't familiar with.

The best way to deal with this type of person According to experts, the best way is to simply listen and then wait until the monologuist requests more inputs. If he didn't ask for input after five minutes, attempt to divert him. It is possible to drop something close to another member of the group. Slowly, you can begin another conversation with the person. Then, begin to let everyone else join in.

7. "Malaprops," also known as "Malaprops" also known as Inappropriate Conversationalists

Malaprops are those who can put a great conversationalist at the brink of patience. They're those who talk in an inappropriate manner and discuss inappropriate subjects. They could turn a positive topic into one, which could cause the conversation to become awkward. Sometimes, they might make the other person uncomfortable by soliciting proof of what they are discussing.

Experts suggest that , in order to combat the negative behavior, it is best to be open and honest. There's no other option except to ask the person to stop. However, it is essential to be sure to ask the malaprops with respect. Instead of saying "Shut down!" or "That's enough," it is more appropriate to say "Please stop", "Let him finish the conversation, please" and "I'm sorry that you (the person speaking) is talking."

Chapter 13: Safety for Small Talk

In the earlier chapters, we discussed the ways that small talks can be extremely beneficial in your development, and how it will help you achieve the success you desire. However, as with all issues in our lives, talking about small things is not without its amount of risks. It's no secret that excessive amounts of a good thing could be a negative thing , and there are a few guidelines to follow while engaging in small-talk.

The next chapter in this series will will look at the different precautions you need to follow to be able to engage in an enjoyable and safe conversation.

Be careful

Small talk can be enjoyable If you are able to engage in informal conversations with trustworthy people. If you meet strangers, you must evaluate their character. You can determine a person's character in a matter of minutes meeting them. You'll be able to determine if they are an ideal candidate and who's not based on the way they communicate with you. If you have doubts or aren't interested, simply inform them that you're late and should be somewhere else. Be very cautious when interacting with strangers, and therefore it is recommended to learn to recognize people.

Take note of your words

If you are meeting people, ensure that you be careful with your words, particularly in the first meeting. You shouldn't try to impress them and push the wrong line. You should not hide any important details about yourself, and expect people to talk about themselves. Consider it this way you must divulge only the information or discuss the things that you're looking for a response to. If you are looking for your name to be their only one, then give them your name, and if you need their contact information you can give them that number. The relationship must be reciprocal throughout and you must be aware whenever you meet strangers for small chats.

Body language

If you are engaging in chats with strangers, it is important to use a friendly or civil manner of speaking. You shouldn't be imposing yourself on others or be a burden to them. It is also important not to get too close to them. They are, after all, strangers, and they don't have any idea who you really are. If you attempt to contact them in a way that is too intense, they may feel dissuaded by your touch or turn the other way. They might attempt to get more comfortable with you, and you could get into trouble.

Also, you should not be too stiff and keep from causing any body aches. Relax your body and mind prior to approaching anyone.

The trick is to keep the balance between them and maintain a relaxed as well as normal facial expression.

Do not use force.

If you are approached by an individual, you should not pressure them to engage with you. If they are responsive, then you're able to continue. If they don't , you're free to proceed. Certain people may be sensitive. And If you bother them for a short time, they may call in security personnel and cause you to be in trouble. If they do not respond to you or respond with an uninspiring response, and then start leaving, then you should be the same.

Do not make the same mistake again.

In times of exuberance, we are prone to repeat ourselves. We forget what we've did a few minutes ago and then repeat it over and over. This can make us appear odd and make the person around you feel uncomfortable. Be aware and keep your eyes on the ball. If you feel at ease or intrigued by the other person , focus on their face and try to not get distracted when speaking to them.

Children who are ill-treated

Although it's good to encourage children to engage in conversation but you should warn your children of the consequences when they talk to strangers. They should be encouraged to engage with children of that are their age or younger than them, and not to anyone who is older than them.

Sometimes , it is okay for them to converse with older people but they need to be warned not to divulge any details, regardless of what another person tells them. It is important to instruct that they should have a nice conversation, and then go away.

Simple is best.

This issue has been addressed previously, but it is important to be repeated. It is essential to keep things simple when making an informal conversation, especially when you are talking to an unknown person. It is enough to make a casual conversation with anyone you think is attractive but that's it. Do not begin with lengthy conversations in order to make them feel special. They won't want to hear your conversation. Engage in a pleasant and enjoyable small talk to build a solid and lasting connection.

Beware of digital chatter

There are times when we want to meet new people via the internet. It's not always the best idea, and it is important to make it a point for yourself and your children to engage in small-scale conversations with each other. It is not advisable to make the new person to your circle and begin chats with them. If you do, it is important to make an effort to be physically present in as many ways as you can. If you just communicate and send messages, then you'll stop living an active social life. It will be easy to become secluded. It is therefore important to step out to meet new people, and enjoy a chat with them.

Avoid bad language

If you meet someone new on the first occasion, and you engage in conversation and conversation, you must ensure that you do not make use of offensive or inappropriate phrases. Don't think of it as appropriate to use profane phrases. It's not fashionable and can deter other person. It is essential to ensure that you don't swear when the person isn't interested in talking with you. Instead, quietly walk away.

If another person is speaking that kind of language just move away. If you talk with them, they may find themselves encouraged to continue.

Chapter 14: Small Talk Etiquette

In addition to the useful guidelines mentioned in preceding chapters, you will need a few guidelines on ways to be aware of when making small talk, especially with those you've just had the pleasure of meeting. To be able to achieve conversational proficiency You should not just learn to communicate and listen with care but be aware of how to conduct yourself in a manner that is appropriate. This chapter will provide tips on proper small talk.

To show respect and politeness towards the person you are communicating with you should take certain steps to follow. The way you conduct yourself plays a major part in conversations. So, it's crucial that you are aware of how to conduct yourself so that you can have an enjoyable and enjoyable conversation, regardless of you're speaking to. Here are some of the guidelines you must keep in mind:

Be informed. It can be difficult to converse with one who doesn't have any knowledge. On the other hand, it's extremely enjoyable to talk to people who are knowledgeable of things. If you are chatting with a friend be sure you're prepared. Be prepared with knowledge about various topics. This will allow you to engage in conversations that are more engaging with your guests and avoid boredom. It's possible to discuss anything that you want, but it is essential to know at least a few topics.

Avoid questions that are personal or about topics. If you don't have a good relationship with the person Do not ask questions about the person's personal life. If you've only been in contact, do not inquire about their family issues, or about the recent heartbreak that he or she has experienced. This will cause them to turn off. Instead, you should start by asking questions that are general.

Leave the conversation courteously. It's rude to simply leave a person when they are still speaking to you regardless of the fact that you have to leave immediately. It won't take too much time when you simply make a statement such as, "Excuse me", or "Thank you for taking the time." Before you end an exchange, ensure that you have permission or excuse yourself, instead of going out at any time you'd like. Be aware that you must always be courteous to the person you are speaking to.

Don't rush. If people are involved in small conversations people tend to be anxious and conscious of how they're acting. Due to this, the tendency is to hurry things along. It is common to ask questions one after another. You start talking quickly and leave your listener confused over what you're talking about. While talking, your conversation must be relaxed, casual and fluid. Be sure to not jump between one subject to the next quickly. Make time to speak about many topics with a relaxed tone.

Be aware. Because you don't know the person as well but, it is crucial to become more aware of his or her feelings and to their desires. It can also be beneficial to pay attention to how you speak as well as the manner in which you speak because you might not be aware that you're coming across as offensive and intimidating. Pay attention to the way someone is acting and look for signs that could indicate the way the person feels or desires. If you feel there's something you can do Do it. Don't sit around waiting for the person to tell you straight in your face that you're insulting them or them or that you are becoming boring and uninteresting to speak to.

Include humor. Humor can help in every conversation. It keeps the conversation lively and enjoyable to engage in. People generally do not enjoy discussions that are serious because, eventually, they become boring. Engaging in serious discussions while adding humor is one of the most entertaining conversations one could ever enjoy. The conversation is casual and intelligent while being a bit sarcastic. It is essential to have laughter in any conversation because serious conversations are boring and boring.

Avoid unsavory gossip and jokes that offend. Even if you don't intend to harm the person you're speaking to, as the two of you making friends it is possible someone else may be confused by the meaning of your joke. If you are looking to bring some humor into the conversation by throwing in jokes ensure that they're not racist, off-color, or offensive. If you are able to make such jokes your audience may be put off by your jokes.

Be sure to keep your information confidential. Even if you haven't established a relationship within your brief conversation ensure that you are aware of what information needs to remain private. You could have earned the confidence of the person you're talking to right away and not even realizing it. That's why they are likely to share their most intimate secrets. You need to be able determine what is to remain private. If someone starts talking about these issues make sure they remain between you and don't divulge to anyone else about what they've disclosed. If you do this it will allow them to be more trusting of you, but you'll also be able to build the relationship you have with them.

Always be grateful. If the person you are talking to is the one who agreed to speak to you, don't forget to thank them for having a great conversation. When you are leaving, tell the person you spoke to that it was a pleasure talking with him or her and that you're looking to speaking to them in the near future. Everyone must observe this act of respect and politeness.

When you remember these points, you'll be able to keep an upbeat mood through the conversation. Additionally, disagreements and miscommunications are prevented. These reminders will assist you to learn to master conversational skills as well as practice small talking. When you practice these skills whenever you're offered the chance it will be a part of your routine.

Chapter 15: Taking It to the Next Level

Socializing can help you make new friends. The first goal is to broaden your circle of friends after which it's only right to move up to a higher degree.

If you've established an excellent rapport with your new acquaintances, it's the time to build lasting relationships, either professionally or personal.

The problem is making simple conversations go into the realm of conversation but the advice in this chapter can help you.

Be Inviting

Many people hate being confined to making small talk with strangers. There's an invisible barrier that their body language create, as if they are you were saying, "Leave me alone, I don't want to bother you."

To build relationships with people the people you want to build relationships with, you must invite people to join you, break down the wall and then let them in.

A body language that is open removes the barriers that prevent people from developing positive relationships with people. Body language includes smiling and displaying an open posture. These gestures indicate that they are welcomed to be close to you.

Don't Judge

The "don't evaluate a book based on its cover" old adage is still relevant. The majority of the time you see people and immediately put them on the table because you don't like how they looked or think that you'll never get along.

They are among the most frequent mistakes made by people. If you judge about someone because of the way they appear, their beliefs differ to yours or they are from different classes of society, you're not giving others an opportunity. You don't want to be judged, do you?

Adjust your mindset. If you're attending an event in which the host is the only person you have ever met Be open to making new acquaintances, but without being judgemental.

Make an effort to meet as many people as you can. Do not stay in one spot. If your host is busy with other guests, it is possible to begin by introductions to other guests.

Keep it Real

If you've ever been at the shopping malls, you've likely been met by someone selling. Salespeople have a knack for attracting people. But, it can be awkward particularly when the first response of the majority of people is to refuse the offer.

It's simple to be more open with people when you trust them to be honest and sincere in their motives. The majority of salespeople visit you for the sake of making friends, but to make a sale.

The most effective salesperson is the one who is authentic and convincing. If you meet an individual, you must be honest. Do not do something because certain people have told you that or the book says to. If you don't have a genuine interest others would be aware and then build walls.

Being authentic is being yourself, not hiding behind pretenses and no lies. Do not embellish your tales, keep your story honest, and eventually you'll be able to see more people attracted by your authenticity.

Don't be afraid to seek help

You can establish a relationship with an individual by asking for help. People like to feel appreciated. If they feel they could be of assistance to you, they'll be there for you without hesitation.

If, for instance, you own an enterprise, you should get feedback from your customers. Accept constructive criticism. Your customers will be grateful to your business for it, causing them to stay with you. The power of asking someone's opinion is powerful. Take advantage of it.

Offer Your Help

Since it's beneficial to seek assistance from others You can also suggest your assistance. It's on both sides: You meet people's needs and feel required, and they satisfy your own need that you feel valued and appreciated.

Similar to you, many people are reluctant to seek help because they fear being judged vulnerable and insecure. This is a way to feed your desire to feel valued and wanted. You may be amazed by the demands of others which can cause you to wonder if this is still true.

However, you should offer assistance without expecting anything in exchange.

Be Personal

The majority of people are able to ensure their professional relationships remain as polished and appropriate in the best way they are able to. If you are trying to maintain acceptable standards of professionalism it is easy to build relationships that tend to be superficial and unauthentic.

Experts believe it's a good idea to establish relationships that are more personal. It means that conversations do not have to be limited to work. Making breaks together. Being able to establish real relationships outside of the workplace.

This is the way you can be in touch and strengthen your bonds and thus forming stronger working relationships.

Agree or disagree

Be honest There will be times when it won't be easy. You will never be able to avoid someone who isn't with you. There will also be people you don't like. If you aren't happy with an idea, state your opinions; don't be averse in order to avoid conflict. It's fine to share your opinion, but make sure you do so with the utmost respect to the person you disagree with.

Do not hesitate to share your views Be prepared to hear other people's views. It is always best to engage in lively discussions with differing opinions. This helps build a stronger bond between those involved in a way that they can resolve every dispute with dignity.

When you're discussing office matters Be aware that it's not always private. Don't take anything personally. That's where the personal connection with your coworkers are crucial. If you're all close friends, you can talk about any topic without having to resent each other when you do not agree with you.

Your friendship with coworkers be natural. If there's one person in your network with whom doesn't share the same kind of personal connection as the others, don't try to force it. Relax and let it happen naturally. The more you chase them the more likely they'll be protected. Be patient, but determined. If they can sense your sincerity, they'll be more opento you, eventually.

Chapter 16: Opinions of Learning

The importance of opinions is a lot for people. People with an introverted personality may keep our opinions to ourselves or perhaps not freely to express opinions. If opinions are voiced, they are often carefully constructed and include a bit of contemplation and a clear viewpoint. If you inquire about their educational background, for instance you're not likely to learn about how they've gotten their college experience, but you'd like to know the reasons they picked a specific school or subject. It is a good idea to ask the person that question instead and it'll lead to a fascinating answer. Look, "why" is a great way to start the sentence since it leaves the person with plenty to talk about. It also makes it appear that you'll be able to understand how their brain functions instead of being able to guess.

You will learn a lot more about the human race by having them explain things to you instead of having to engage in something you may even find both you hate.

You can also determine by the opinions of others whether dating someone is unproductive or beneficial for you. Alex discovered himself in this scenario, but Alex was pleasantly surprised to find out that the sole reason for his future girlfriend to go to the college she attended was due to the fact that it allowed her to get away from her home and she was enthralled by her independence. She could have gone to the better school close to home, but Alayna [KFW4] wanted to live her the world without parents overseeing her every move. This was a nice thing to think to know because Alex is also awed with the same degree of freedom. They shared interests, and Alex knew that their relationship would flourish.

If you are forced to elaborate on what you do, look at acknowledgement and praise. This can provide you with a good idea of how the person you're communicating with is excited by the things you've said. Perhaps, for instance, you ran today. It's not a big thing to talk about however, if you do, observe the reaction. It is easy to tell from tiny reaction (looking to their drink, glancing away, or their face changed to one of disinterest.) whether they're bored with "fitness crazy" or if they have the same enthusiasm that you have for self-care. You should be prepared to share some small conversation to keep the flow of conversation flowing but it's not necessary to be a long-distance conversation. When you're just beginning to meet people a bit more intimately and feel comfortable sharing your personal details with them the conversations you have with them may require some unnecessary small conversation.

Be honest in situations when you are feeling that your conversation isn't getting you in the direction you'd like. For instance If you're talking to a girl about parties, but you're not a party person Let her know right from the beginning that you're not one of them. Honesty is important because during small talk people are likely to try to make you look attractive. Perhaps they don't have a lot of fun or even believe that it makes them appear exciting and enjoyable. If you don't want to let them go along with something which doesn't appeal to you in any way you can cut them off by letting them speak a some honesty. This can help bring the conversation back to its original purpose and help you focus on topics that are more interesting to you.

Say it!

* I don't really like camping.
* I really don't like gatherings.
* Huge crowds aren't my style.
* I'm not a fan of sports in any way. It's pointless.

There is no need to engage in lots of conversation in the event that you're open about your feelings. For instance, you can simply let them know that you prefer to be intimate, rather than the busy scenes. That will set the stage for a successful relationship since that could be the goal they were trying to reach in the first place. Even in the unlikely scenario where the relationship is not successful or is never able to happen the relationship remains authentic and real. It is better to get these issues off the table early so that you don't are caught in the middle of a long-running relationship rife with lies and flimsy and for some, it is a lot worse that being rejected. It's true.

If you're looking to be honest keep in mind that many like this approach since it offers them the chance to break the Ice in a more efficient method. There are opinions out there and you've been sincere, and they won't have to wait for a long time before you open the door and share information about your character. It's far better to conduct things this way, especially if you are sure that having an honest, long-term genuine relationship is what you want to achieve. [KFW5]

Keep your word, be honest, and remain loyal and let the bond begin. It's important to practice honesty in order to connect with people who are like you at the top of the list. Honesty (not excessively obviously, but not like Rami Malek's character in Mr. Robot) will get you to where you're supposed to be. Try it! [KFW6]

Chapter 17: Time for The Talking Bit

Here's how we dive into the essential. We've covered the mind, communication through body language, and being authentic, none of that have anything to do with speaking in actual terms. We're now on to the only step that isn't natural and falls in the "learned ability" category. This is purely repetition and memorization. It can be difficult to keep these topics in mind and conversation starters can be difficult when you're uncomfortable, shy, and on the on the spot. This is where the difficulty lies.

The benefit of having a few good conversations is that you are able to take a cue from them. If the conversation becomes uncomfortable or slows down it is possible to pull out one of these topics and make sure you keep the conversation for another few minutes.

There are millions of these , instead of listing the various ideas for conversation starting points and general subjects. I'm going to break down the characteristics that define a great one and what makes a poor one, to aid you in creating the perfect list of your own. Before we dive into the details but, I'd like to clarify that I do not believe that it's identical to an actual conversation topic. Conversation starters for me are the phrases are used to begin the conversation, which implies that you've not yet begun to talk to the person you are talking to. Conversation topics are the phrases or questions that you ask to keep conversation going.

Bad conversation starters

If you search "conversation starters" there are a number of them that are not very good and some of them aren't even starters at all, but rather subjects that you might be able to bring up during the course of conversations. I'd like to share the reason why these are bad so you can come up with excellent conversation starters and not be stuck with these types of topics.

The first one that is not good is to make comments about weather. They aren't good, but I've used them in dire situations, but I have also seen them quickly shift the topic into something that is more intriguing. Example:

Me: "man it sure is the day that it is raining!"

Another individual: "sure is, downpouring."

This is the point where the conversation can end up dying an unintentional death. This is why this conversation starter is dangerous unless you're on your feet and ready to save the situation. I'm not a fan of putting me in situations that I'm required to save something from high in my list, and I always make an effort to stay clear of the weather-related comments. Plus I'll tell you how I'd handle this conversation.

Another individual: "sure is, downpouring."

I: "All the more reason to go to Mexico! There's a reason why I always find myself booking my vacations in the summer , but the spring rainy season is the time I should be taking advantage of it. Do you agree?"

We can now start discussing vacation plans. Conversations is saved, but not so easily.

Another conversation starter that isn't a good idea is a very generic one such as "What's the story behind you?" or "Tell me about your life?" These are bad because they're way too general and place the person in the middle. If you were to actually say these things in a conversation someone, they'd find you odd. Which is your experience? Who would you say that to. Be careful not to create a conversation starter that is too personal or vague.

Another bad question is "do do you subscribe to podcasts? If so? If so, what's your favourite?" Now I know I mentioned earlier that you shouldn't make questions unclear, however questions with too much detail can be poor. There are many people who listen to podcasts. The reply to that question could possibly be "no I don't listen to any." The conversation has ended and you must save the conversation with a different question. This type of question can be utilized as a topic of conversation when you've been talking to someone for time and need to find something to keep the conversation going. If they state that they don't use podcasts for listening, then you could suggest a podcast you like and believe they would like. It's much simpler to accomplish if you've already been talking and discovered a few things about them.

Good conversation starters

The most effective conversation starters are actually easy and natural. They're not expensive. They're dull and boring and that's why they are amazing. They can be used in any circumstance to start a conversation. Remember, the term "conversation starter" is not an issue you can pose midway in a conversation, so it can continue to flow. This is why questions like "what are you doing to spend your time?" make no sense. What do you think it will take to meet someone and begin with them in that manner? The majority of the conversation starters I have seen online are far too specific.

It's great to test and connect your conversation starters with your favorite subjects so that you can further expand the topics you like. For example , any mention of films or filmmaking is an excellent one for me as I was employed within the field of film and was enthusiastic about making films. Be sure to tailor your conversation starters reflect your preferences. Here are some examples of real conversation starters that you could make use of to begin a conversation with anyone.

"Hey I'm Lana I don't think we've ever met."

"Hey What type of beer (or another drink) is it? I don't believe I've tried it" or "nice that what you're sipping (insert drink) it's my favorite I'm a big fan of IPAs"

"Hey we haven't spoken to you in several months, what's happening? Are you still working in the same spot?"

"Hey me and my buddy were engaged in a discussion on the most excellent eatery in the area Do you have a favourite?" If they say not, ask if they've been around the city for a long time or just relocated.

Comment or questions regarding the surroundings. Things like "this convention centre is massive wouldn't it?" or "Bob's house is gorgeous, isn't? I've never been to this place before."

And so on. The most important thing is to be aware that the conversation starters you pick should be straightforward and appropriate to nearly every scenario. They can be open-ended, but precise enough that they don't make the other person feel on the spot.

The conversation will continue to flow

The best method to keep the conversation going is to inquire about what someone else mentioned, but at times that conversation gets stale and it's impossible to save it. That's when you can choose a conversation subject that is usually referred to as being a "conversation starter" but really serves as the best way to keep an already established conversation. These topics are also most effective in the context of your own interests. These are just a few examples of this:

Have you seen any great films recently?

Are you planning anything for this weekend?

Any vacations scheduled in the near time?

Did you hear about the latest news story on [insert topic here]Did you hear about [insert latest news topic]?

The best part about these questions is that even if your response is "no" it's likely that they're going to ask whether you've watched an excellent film or have plans for the weekend, etc. This is the reason you need the answer to these in your head , so that you are able to keep discussing them and then respond to questions if they weren't able to provide an answer. This is a method to make sure that you are foolproof with your conversations since you are able to discuss them. Do not ask a question to which you don't know the answer for yourself.

There's nothing wrong having an "go-to" story

I was within the field of film for several years, and the business I worked at was continuously trying for new clients. My boss had the potential to be the winner of gold in"the small-talk" Olympics One of his strategies was to use a standard story. I frequently watched him tell the same story to potential clients, and they would even repeat entire conversations using the exact same jokes. He would often recount these tales repeatedly but only to those he'd only had a conversation with. Even though these stories seemed boring to me but anyone he'd been speaking to was always awed.

My boss told I that it's always a great practice to have a tale that you can always pull from your pockets even if you know that your closest acquaintances have heard of it before. If the person you're communicating with hasn't heard about the story, take it out and start the conversation.

Share some compliments

A note of caution: you must keep your tone subtle. Don't overdo it by showering the recipient with accolades. Be careful not to appear uncomfortable or unfriendly. If you see someone who is friendly to waiters, begin your conversation by saying something like, "It's rare to find people who treat waiters so well and, by the way, my name is _____. What's your day like?" What did I say? When you have praised someone, don't be stuck. You should quickly move on from the praise , and then continue with casual questions regarding the weather conditions, their location or the way their day is coming out.

Certain people aren't at ease with being acknowledged and may be a bit frightened them to learn that someone is offering them an appreciation. If you can shift the conversation to something else, they will feel at ease. This way, it won't become uncomfortable and gives time for the person who is giving you the compliment to digest the compliment. It's a nice way to communicate with the person you are communicating with.

They are also a lot more easy to incorporate into conversations that are already taking place, rather than claiming as a way to start a conversation. A comment such as "that's hilarious, you're hilarious!" "yeah that's true that you're really clever" can sound more authentic if made in a casual way.

We've now gone over the general mindset you must take to be able to master small talking. In the following chapters I'll highlight the most frequent situations in which you'll need these skills as well as specific techniques you'll need to master in these situations.

Chapter 18: Preparing Your Mind with a Positive Attitude

It's probably not an amazement to you to know that the concept of inspiration is typically at the center in positive research on the brain.

It's not always about simply smiling and being energetic; it is more often about one's overall perspective on life and their tendency to focus on everything that is normal in everyday life.

In this article we'll discuss the basic principles of positive brain research, and identify a fraction of the numerous benefits that come from living your life from an optimistic perspective and explore some suggestions and techniques for cultivating an attitude of inspiration.

What is a positive mindset and Attitude?

It's possible to already have an idea that a positive attitude or an inspiring attitude looks like today but it's always beneficial to start with the definition.

"Positive thinking is mental and enthusiastic attitude that focuses on the bright aspect of life and anticipates positive results."

A further definition that is progressively more comprehensive is:

"Positive reasoning is the process of taking on life's challenges from an optimistic perspective. It's not necessarily about keeping an eminent separation from or absconding with the negative aspects of life; instead it's about making the most of potentially traumatic circumstances, and trying to see the good in the world around you, and looking at yourself and your capabilities positively."

We can infer from these definitions and come up with an accurate description of a positive attitude as the ability to look upon the positive side of things, look forward to positive outcomes, and approach challenges through an optimistic view.

A positive outlook means creating a positive mindset and always looking for the silver lining and making the most out of whatever situation you are in.

Six examples of qualities and traits of a positive Mental State

As we have come to appreciate what positive thinking is and what it is, we can now tackle the most important question What is it that it resembles? There are many characteristics and qualities that are associated with positive thinking, for example:

Positive thinking: the ability to give an attempt and take on a risk instead of assuming that your effort won't yield results.

Acknowledgement: accepting that things aren't always working out the way you want you to, and yet learning from your mistakes.

The concept of reversibility is to avoid frustration, discomfort, or frustration, rather than giving up.

Appreciation: consistently, effectively appreciating the things that are useful throughout your life (Blank 2017, 2017).

Cognizance/Mindfulness: devoting the brain to cognizant mindfulness and improving the capacity to center.

Honesty is the trait of being honest, upright and straight instead of being enticing and auto-focused (Power of Positivity, n.d.).

These are not the only characteristics of a positive mind but they could also work in the opposite direction, effectively accepting hopefulness, acknowledgement and appreciation, strength as well as trustworthiness within your own life will help you in creating and keeping your positive attitude.

The A-List Of Positive Attitudes

If you find the information above to be too vague There are many more explicit examples of a positive attitude in the real world.

Examples of inspirational perspectives could be:

It's a way of looking at difficulties without hesitation... And laughing.

You get what you pay for and not yelling.

The ability to make a profit out of the unplanned or unexpected in the event that it's not what required initially.

Inspire everyone around you with Positive words.

Utilizing the force of a smile to change around the mood of a situation.

You are invited to a party for which where you don't even have the slightest idea of.

It's the process of getting back up every time you fall. (Regardless of how often you fall.)

Being a fountain of energy that inspires others around you.

Knowing that connections are a more important thing than things.

Be positive in every situation is a good thing, even when you've got almost nothing.

Making memories that last a lifetime in any situation even if you're losing.

Feeling happy for the other person's happiness.

A positive vision for the future regardless of your current circumstances.

Smiling.

A acknowledgement even to an outsider.

Let someone know that they did an excellent job. (Also do not make fun over this.)

A smile that fills someone's heart. (Not just youngsters... adults also want their day to be memorable, too!)

It's not complaining regardless of how untrue it is. Things have all the hallmarks of being. (It is a exercise in defeat... rather do something!)

Beware of letting the cynicism of others make you feel like a failure.

More than you think to receive in return.

Be realistic about you... always

Why is an attitude of positivity considered to be the most important factor to succeed?

Today, we are learning more concerning what having a good attitude can look like. It is possible to answer the most important question about what's the deal when you have a positive mindset?

What is it about having an optimistic view of that is significant and so efficient, as well as revolutionary?

Indeed, the characteristics and characteristics listed above offer a hint of what to expect. If you look through the written material, you'll find numerous advantages linked to strength, idealism, and concern.

It's clear that trustworthiness and mindfulness are linked to greater satisfaction in life, and acknowledgement and appreciation can move you from living the "alright lifestyle" towards "easy road."

The significance of developing the right Thoughts

It is important to develop a truly positive attitude, and picking these benefits is a part of the thinking you create. PsyCap was first conceived of to be "positive mental capital" by highly regarded authorities and administration analyst Luthans as well as Youssef at the time of 2004. The concept quickly gained traction with positive authoritative analysts and by 2011 , there were numerous instances to PsyCap on paper.

The first meta-examination to begin the study of PsyCap was conducted in the year 2011, and highlighted some of the many benefits of PsyCap within the workplace:

* PsyCap is adamantly associated as a source of fulfillment in work, authoritative responsibility, and mental health.

* PsyCap was also linked to hierarchical civics (alluring employees to engage in practices) and various levels of performance (self-appraised and manager evaluations and targets).

* PsyCap was negatively associated as having negative feelings, a desire to increase turnover stress, work pressure, and anxiety.

* PsyCap was similarly negatively associated with negative representative aberration (awful work methods; Avey, Reichard, Luthans, and Mhatre 2011,).

It seems to be obvious that inspirational views such as confidence and courage will result in positive results both for the association and the employees!

Another study by a handful of mammoths from the area of positive brain research (Sonja Lyubomirsky Laura King, and Ed Diener in 2005) examined the link between happiness and benefits to employees. They found that positive mental states in the workplace benefit the employee, despite the connection:

* Employees who are more joyful have higher earnings than other employees.
* Sales reps who are cheerful are more successful as compared to other sales representatives.
* Happy employees are more ingenious than different people.
* Employees who are chummy are rated in a more stern manner in the eyes of their managers.
* People who are upbeat are less likely to exhibit their withdrawal from work (non-appearance and turnover, burnout and retaliatory behavior).
* Upbeat employees have more cash flow than workers of other types.

In this way, a positive outlook can provide a wealth of advantages for the organization as a whole and also for its employees.

* Note the true and the great in the midst of disaster and adversity.

Make arrangements in case you have to raise concerns.

* Make someone smile.

Finally the 11 methods of Tchiki Davis, Dr. Tchiki Davis (2018) will also assist you in adopting a more inspirational attitude:

* Consider asking you, "Do I think emphatically?" Test yourself or take a test your inspiration to determine where you are.

* Refresh your memory for positive information by using positive phrases more frequently.

Increase your cerebrum's ability to process positive thoughts by incorporating practices which include positive phrases.

• Increase the capacity of your cerebrum to concentrate on the positive by regularly redirecting your attention away from the negative and towards the positive.

You can prepare yourself to experience random moments of energy (utilize the traditional mold on yourself to build positive connections).

* Be positive, but not all that much, and consider negative thoughts when you have to. Here and there we must lament and think about the negative effects and use

negative feelings to draw and convince into us.

* Practise appreciation (maybe with an appreciation journal).
* Applaud the high points (stop for a moment to "enjoy the ambience" and praise your positive).
* Create positive feelings by watching funny videos

Stop focusing on your wins and acknowledge the effort that you have put into.

It's time to stop all-or-nothing thinking. this kind of psychological bend isn't a reflection of reality because things happen occasionally "all wonderful" or "all awful."

Chapter 19: What to Do and Don't's to Avoid When You Talk To A Stranger

It isn't a matter of how many effective opening lines you've got in your wallet If you're not aware of the rules of communicating with people you don't are familiar with. You can't expect everyone will share your sense of humor , or appreciate your jokes. It's more challenging when you don't have a relationship with the person and, more importantly, you don't know the indicators for certain subjects. However, we're much closer than we imagine and there's some things we all love and dislike when talking to people on the first date. Learn them all by heart and you'll stay safe from getting exiled from the most attractive club.

Let's start with the positive suggestions. Make use of them as often as you can and commit yourself to making a positive first meeting. Here are some things to do when you are attempting to talk with someone who you don't know:

1. Smile! It is a gesture that will open up any heart Don't forget to make this kind gesture of kindness.

2. Represent yourself by stating your name. In the end, who cares what you're going to say if someone doesn't know the proper way to address you.

3. Tell a funny story that makes the person you are talking to smile. Jokes can be a great method of breaking an ice among two people and laughter can be a great starting point for any conversation.

4. Ask the questions of your partner Show that you're curious about their interests or occupation, their life style, etc.

5. Listen at what someone else has to say. this is a great skill since, on the one hand, it provides more information about the person and also make it clear that you're keen to hear the things they say.

6. Respect the boundaries of your partner This is an crucial point to make. There is always a certain amount of caution when speaking to strangers , so don't cut the

physical distance between you simultaneously. It is a hassle and likely, conversations will be unattainable within a matter of minutes. Another important thing to remember is to pay attention to what you say. Be mindful of the selection of topics and words as there are some people who are sensitive to certain subjects. If, for instance, you meet someone who is attractive, charming, and beautiful slim lady, there's no way to discuss the latest method to lose weight is it not?

7.Make subtle compliments . There is nothing more pleasing than a classy and classy compliment, regardless of the recipient, whether either a woman or a man. Be sure to compliment the choice of accessories such as "Great choice of colour for your dress, it compliments your skin tone perfect" and "That is an excellent watch You can tell you're a man with style".

8.Feel free to change your subject at the point that the silence is uncomfortable - instead of using catchy phrases such as "um" as well as "huh" or trying to think of a way to think of an appropriate phrase, simply switch the subject.

9.Tell short stories based on personal experiences. Stick to those that are humorous and entertaining. Use them as an impromptu joke. The possibility of making jokes about yourself indicates that you're confident enough and you're not scared of the smallest incidents.

10. Do not let others interrupt you when you're talking. This is not an indication of disrespect, but it indicates that they are impressed by what you're talking about and want to learn more of your thoughts on the subject.

Then we must go on with the don't section of the chapter.

1.Don't discuss only yourself. A person who doesn't know you does not need to be bombarded by all the details of your life. You'll bore them to death and be called a bore.

2.Don't talk about persons in the room This is a huge mistake. Are you thinking that people who do not know one another gather in one location to discuss the opinions of others? This happens only when you're an intimate group of people. It is possible to make nice remarks regarding someone else, but do not use negative terms. It is a sign of bad taste and is considered to be low-class.

3.Don't look at someone else's shoulder you're talking to . This is the best way to show that you don't appreciate the person in front of you. This is a snide way to do even when in a conversation with a friend and even when you are trying to impress someone new. It only sends one message "I am speaking to you, but I'm looking for someone who is more intriguing".

4.Don't focus on just one subject . This is boring and it's possible that the person isn't interested in the subject at all. Therefore, he may be nice enough to be being listened to for 5-10 minutes, but at the end they'll be searching for a way to escape from you.

5.Don't give out any personal details with strangers. Of course it's necessary to share your personal information, including your occupation, and hobbies. However, telling anyone who you have met in the beginning you're experiencing a divorce that is not a good one or you suffer from some health issue (if not specifically asked about it) could make them feel uncomfortable and uncertain of what to do. It is something that should be shared with the people who are affected by the same situation and who can help you in a way.

6.Don't make racist religious, explicit sexual or stereotype jokes. You aren't aware of the history and the source of the person you are talking to. Don't risk putting each of them in a embarrassing situation. In particular, do not ridicule people who are blonde, Jewish persons, Afro-Americans gay, homosexuals or lesbians, etc. Even if the person you are referring to isn't one of them but he may have an intimate friend or relative that belongs to any of the groups. Furthermore, certain people may feel strongly negative to jokes like these.

7.Don't be critical and pick on other people - if you do this, someone who does not realize that you are doing it will believe you are someone who only sees bad things about other people. Nobody likes people who think they're more superior than the rest of the world.

8. Don't discuss money. It does not matter if you have the money or don't. Nobody cares about your financial situation and truthfully, it's not something to discuss even with your friends.

9.Don't ever ever ask the following questions to a stranger There are a few phrases that can get you kicked out of the conversation immediately: "Are you married?", "How is your husband or wife performing?", "How much is your income?". Do we have to justify why ? Just think of getting a divorce when you discover your spouse is in a relationship with someone else, and then losing your job and having the burden of a loan and child care pay.

10. Do not try to force engaging in conversation If it's clear that the person

isn't keen on it It's not worth it to be imaginative and clever and just take a take a step back. It is best to be able to accept that it's not personaland they're not ready to engage with strangers.

We also divide what you should and shouldn't do when you are talking to strangers in the beginning. It is important to remember you are not allowed to break these guidelines. If you adhere to these guidelines You can be certain that your first interaction with someone new will go well.

Conclusion

I am very excited to share this information to you. I am extremely happy to have learned and may be able to apply these methods in the future.

I hope this book has been useful in helping you comprehend how you can also light discussions and make new acquaintances and business connections.

It is the next thing to do: start by using this information, and hopefully lead a happier life. You will be able to enjoy the many new people you meet!

If you know someone who could benefit from the advice provided here , please tell them about this book.

Thanks and best of luck!

www.ingramcontent.com/pod-product-compliance
Lightning Source LLC
Chambersburg PA
CBHW071842080526
44589CB00012B/1086